LESLEY FORREST

A HEALTHY START

SIMPLE WHOLEFOOD RECIPES FOR BABIES AND YOUNG CHILDREN

ANDRE DEUTSCH

To Jeremy and Nat

First published in Great Britain 1990
by André Deutsch Limited
105–106 Great Russell Street London WC1B 3LJ

ISBN 0 233 98549 2
ISBN 0 233 98568 9 (paperback edition)

Printed in Great Britain by
WBC Limited, Bristol

CONTENTS

A practical, simple and imaginative cookbook for the busy parent who wants her children brought up on *real* food has long been needed. Too much vague advice about vitamins, minerals and feeding your children well has led to a lot of confusion in the minds of busy parents wanting to do the best for their families. This is because the real issue of *how* is seldom addressed.

Lesley Forrest rises beautifully to the challenge. She has produced truly simple yet delicious recipes using unadulterated, nutritious, fresh foods. She tells you clearly how to prepare children's meals with the kind of care that will preserve their value and she makes the whole process fun.

The recipes for fruit purécs for small babies through dishes made of grains, pulses, vegetables, chicken and fish have all been devised personally, lovingly for her own son. This brings an important extra dimension to the book for as a busy mother she is well aware of the challenges every parent faces such as: What foods do you use in weaning a young baby? How do you offer sweets that are nourishing and won't destroy teeth? What food additives should you absolutely avoid if you are concerned about protecting the long term health of your child?

She even deals with the question of combining different vegetarian foods such as pulses and grains to ensure that your child gets the full spectrum of essential amino acids which is vital to his good physical and mental development. Every recipe is designed in quantity to serve one adult and one child which means that the single parent can make good use of it without continual mathematical calculations.

A Healthy Start is a book I can highly recommend. I am very much looking forward to its sequel.

Leslie Kenton

Why I Have Written this Book

By the time I had my son, Nat, cooking without meat had become second nature to me. I stopped eating meat, for ethical reasons, some eight years earlier and had been pleasantly surprised to find how easy it was to eat well without it – especially since we continued to enjoy fish.

It was not until I began weaning Nat that I realized how little practical guidance was available on feeding babies and young children without meat. Like many new parents, I became pre-occupied with my child's eating habits and, in the process of working out a balanced diet for him, I began to formulate what constituted healthy eating for a growing child.

Sensible parents are rightly concerned about what their children are eating, whether or not they are vegetarian. It is not only growing public awareness of the suffering of factory-farmed animals, but also an increased understanding of the relationship between diet and disease and worries about the effects on our health of too much refined and processed food which have prompted a widespread interest in healthy eating and a steady decrease in meat consumption.

As I was adapting and experimenting with recipes for my son, it occurred to me to offer my collection as inspiration for all those parents who want healthy children with a taste for good food! While my recipes show how unnecessary meat is for a healthy diet, they will also provide variety in the diet of those children whose parents, while still eating meat, are cutting down on it. I have included a few free-range chicken recipes for those who, while giving up red meat, continue to eat poultry.

My Approach to Food

I believe that children's food should be unadulterated, nutritious, fresh and delicious. I also feel it should be prepared with the same care that we adults give our own food. Indeed, from the very start, I tasted everything I cooked for Nat – after all, if I thought it was disgusting, why on earth should he like it?

On this basis, what is good enough for my child must be good enough for me (with a little extra seasoning) and most of my recipes are designed for two people – the cook and the child. This not simply because it is easier to cook for two but also because I think that it is positively good to eat with your children whenever you can. While proper family meals may not be possible during the week, at least you can sit down with your child – eating, after all, should be a social activity not a lonely chore.

My recipes demonstrate that a meat-free, wholefood diet (which includes fish) is rich in all a growing child needs. And, because you will probably have given it more thought than the meals reluctantly churned out from the 'meat and two veg' school of cookery, it will also be more interesting.

The right food builds healthy children; it also contributes to an amiable temperament. A wide variety of food encourages experimentation and an enjoyment of different tastes. Good eating patterns, established early, are rewarding for the parent and satisfying for the child. Later these will enable the child himself to tell the difference between real food and unhealthy imitations (despite some inevitable detours into junk food on the way!).

A Healthy Diet

Nutritionalists have long agreed that a healthy diet is one containing a high proportion of wholegrain cereals, fresh fruit and vegetables. They agree that we should eat more healthy oils – from fish, vegetables, nuts and seeds – and less unhealthy saturated fats of the kind found in animal and dairy products. They advise that we reduce our intake of salt and sugar. While all this is important for adults, it is critical for the health of growing children. The maxim 'eat fresh, eat wholefood' more or less sums it up!

Wholefoods are exactly what their name suggests: those foods which come to us as nature intended with their full complement of vitamins, minerals, fibre, protein and essential oils still intact. This means wholegrains (and the foods made from them like wholemeal flour, wholemeal bread, wholewheat pasta etc), seeds and pulses, as well as fresh fruit and vegetables.

Much manufactured food, in the process of being refined and preserved, has had healthy fibre and many of its important nutrients removed. In other words, its goodness has largely disappeared. In many cases, what we are left with are various combinations of refined starches and sugars glued together with saturated fats. These are then preserved, flavoured and coloured by chemicals.

Food additives in the UK remain poorly controlled and inadequately tested. Many are still not revealed on food labels, and some known to cause toxic effects continue to be approved by the Government. For a summary of those additives which it is recommended that you avoid giving your babies and children, see Appendix pp. 123–4.

Combining Proteins

When people first cut down on or eliminate meat from their diet, they often worry about eating sufficient protein, particularly if they are feeding growing children.

However, it is reassuring to know that, even if you eliminate all animal and fish protein, you are left with more than enough high-quality protein in vegetable foods. All cereals, as well as fruit and vegetables, contain some protein, as well as the more obvious 'high protein' foods like pulses, nuts and seeds. And, of course, dairy produce is full of it.

The only significant difference between animal and vegetable protein is not one of quality but 'ease of use'. While the body can directly use meat because it is a 'complete' protein, the protein in plants is not usually complete in this way. Vegetable proteins need to be combined (ie eaten together in a meal) so that what one lacks the other provides and together they complement each other to give a complete protein which the body can use efficiently.

All this really means is that, to get the most value out of your food, certain combinations are better than others. But which?

In a vegetarian diet, apart from fruit and vegetables, there are four main categories of food which should be included in a balanced diet: 1) Grains (eg rice, wheat); 2) Pulses (eg kidney beans, lentils); 3) Seeds (eg sesame, peanuts); and 4) Dairy products (eg milk, eggs). The foods which complement each other and together provide the basis of a balanced meal are shown in the simple diagram opposite.

The combinations indicated by straight lines are the most reliable ones. By combining foods from these categories, eg pulses with grain, we increase by over one third the amount of protein our bodies can use. The zig-zag lines indicate that some, but not all, foods from these categories complement each other.

Don't worry if this explanation still leaves you confused: if

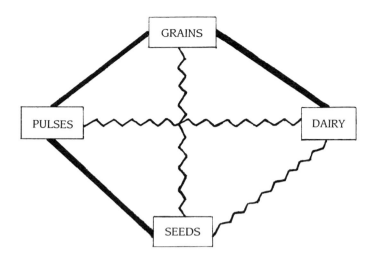

you follow the recipes in this book and serve them with the suggested accompaniments, you will not even have to think about combining proteins. 'Complementarity' is built into them all.

Sugar

I know it is extremely hard to resist giving your child sweet things – there are all sorts of pressures, not least among them the feeling that you are somehow unfairly depriving your child of a treat. However, especially in a child's first few years, the longer you can keep sugar away from him the better.

The earlier a child gets a sweet tooth, the more difficult it will be to prevent him having distressing dental work, even on his milk teeth, and being unduly addicted to sugar for the rest of his life. The process begins with jars of unsuitable baby food like 'chocolate dessert' and continues through biscuits, cakes, ice-creams and sweets, all of which fuel an addiction to sugar and ruin a child's appetite.

Apart from those products which obviously contain sugar (like fizzy drinks and desserts) there is also concealed sugar in a wide variety of processed foods from soups and sauces to tinned vegetables and breakfast cereals.

The alternatives are healthy snacks like fresh fruits, cheese, dried fruits or wholemeal scones, and 'treats' such as the home-made desserts or milk-shakes given here, using only good ingredients with a minimum of natural sweetening (fruit purées, fruit juice, honey). If you are going to give sweet things it is a good idea to reserve them for after a meal – a child will then get into the habit of filling up on proper food first. Dentists say that eating sugar in this way, at one sitting, is far less harmful to the teeth than sucking at sweets several times a day.

Free-Range Eggs and Salmonella Poisoning

A major source of salmonella food poisoning – now a serious problem in the UK – is contaminated eggs. Without going into the reasons for this here, there are certain basic things you should do to avoid this infection, which can be serious, if not fatal, amongst vulnerable groups. These include babies and pregnant women.*

When buying eggs do note the following:

1. Pay no attention to any claims that flocks of laying hens are salmonella-free.

2. Battery eggs are no safer than free-range eggs.

* See Dr Richard Lacey, *Safe Shopping, Safe Cooking, Safe Eating* (Penguin: London, 1989).

3. Eggs should be stored at room temperature in shops.
4. Always check the sell-by date.
5. Examine each egg and reject any which are cracked or covered in droppings.
   At home:
1. Do *not* store eggs in the fridge.
2. Cook eggs until the yolk is pale yellow and firm. Well-cooked scrambled eggs, omelettes and soufflés should be relatively safe; ordinary cooking of fried and poached eggs is unlikely to kill salmonella bacteria.
3. Do not eat raw eggs.
4. None of this is absolutely foolproof, so sadly it is not advisable to give any eggs to babies under a year old.
   For advice on salmonella and listeria in chicken see p. 88.

Quantities

All recipes are for one adult and one child unless otherwise stated.

EARLY
BEGINNINGS:
PUREES

There is no doubt that 'breast is best' as a sure foundation for your baby's good health; nothing else can provide the same level of immunity against infection and disease. However, if breast-feeding is not possible or desired, there are perfectly adequate substitutes available (choose milk formulas with a low aluminium content).

The right moment for introducing 'solids' will depend entirely on you and your baby – my son, at a birth weight of over 11 lbs, needed a supplement to my milk at $2\frac{1}{2}$ months but this is unusually early; somewhere between 3 and 6 months is more common!

While tinned and packet baby foods can be terribly useful when you are in a hurry, overtired, or going abroad, I do recommend that you try to start your baby off on your own purées. You can never be sure of the quality of processed foods (meat products, for example, can legally contain offal, feet and testicles; vegetable foods can be bulked up with cheap thickeners), while you know exactly what is in your own cooking. If you do use processed foods, make sure that they are free from additives, preservatives and artificial colourants.

There are some minor differences in opinion about which particular foods are the best to start your baby off with, but there is general agreement about the basic principles involved. Salt, salty foods (like yeast extract), and heavy spices should be avoided for the first year; and sugar should only be used sparingly, if at all. Foods which are difficult to digest or commonly induce allergic reactions should also be avoided in the early months. These are known to include bottled cow's milk (a child must be at least 6 months before he drinks this), egg white, wheat (this contains 'gluten'), nuts, tomatoes and some soft fruits like strawberries. In the light of recent information about salmonella it would, unfortunately, be wise not to give eggs to babies under one year old in any circumstances. For advice on giving eggs to children, see Introduction p. 6.

It is not difficult to prepare fresh baby foods, especially since many purées are suitable for the freezer and can be frozen in tiny convenient quantities – for example, in the ice tray. Once it is full, flip out the contents and transfer into labelled bags. When needed, cubes are quickly defrosted and only minimal amounts are wasted. A food processor is too large to cope with such small amounts of food – your baby's lunch ends up wrapped entirely around the blades – so it is worth buying or borrowing a hand blender.

Always choose ripe fruits and firm vegetables; favour whole-grain cereals unless there is a reason not to; sweeten with natural ingredients (fruit purées or juice) rather than sugar, and make sure pulses and grains are properly cooked. I started my son on purées made from fresh fruits, palatable vegetables, brown rice cereal and easily digestible pulses.

Avocado Purée

In season, avocados can be quite cheap. A hard, unripe pear is inedible, so choose those which are soft to the gentle pressure of your thumb at the very top of the fruit. Avocados are bland, wonderfully nutritious and easily digested – in fact, a perfect baby food!

Scoop the flesh out of half an avocado, remove any black or stringy bits, and blend or mash well with a fork. Use the remaining half as quickly as possible but, in the meantime, keep in the fridge with the stone in it, covered tightly with clingfilm.

Mashed Banana

It is a rare baby that does not like the naturally sweet taste of bananas. They are full of minerals, carbohydrates and vitamin C, and a reliable first food. Make sure, however, that they are very ripe, choosing those whose skins are beginning to turn black.

Peel the banana and mash well with a fork. (Some people like to take out the central seeds to start with but I certainly did not find this necessary.)

Apricot and Apple Purée

Both of these fruits can, of course, be served on their own but since apricot purée is a good freezer food, it is easy enough to combine the two as well. Apples contain vitamins, essential acids and minerals, while dried apricots are especially rich in iron. Dried fruit which has been treated with chemicals (avoid sulphur dioxide E220) before drying and then coated in mineral oil (which retards the absorption of vitamins) should be washed in hot water before use. If possible, buy fruit which has been naturally dried and is unsulphured – more likely the Australian and Californian brands. These need only be rinsed in cold water before soaking.

Rinse the dried apricots, then cover with cold water and soak overnight. (I do this even when the packet says it is not required.) Then simmer gently in the same water for about 25 minutes or until they are very soft and pulpy. Cool and blend. Freeze in tiny meal-size quantities (eg in an ice tray).

For apple purée, use sweet eaters, not cooking apples which require lots of added sugar. Peel and core. If they are really sweet, you can grate the raw apple on the fine side of a grater to give a mushy pulp – use immediately, before it discolours. Otherwise, cook the sliced apple in a little water or apple juice until it disintegrates. Cool and blend.

First Cereal: Brown Rice

It is advisable to begin with rice and progress slowly through the other cereals – barley, millet, corn, oats and, finally, wheat. Many children have an allergic reaction to the gluten in wheat, which is why it is usually wise to delay its introduction. Unless there is some medical reason to avoid wholegrains, I would start as you mean to go on, beginning with ground brown rice.

There is no need to mess around grinding your own grains since health food shops sell pre-ground brown rice which is simple to prepare.

As a rule of thumb, use about 1 heaped teaspoon of rice flour to 4 fl. oz of milk (breast or formula milk until about 6 months old). Mix the gently warmed milk slowly into the flour to make a paste, gradually adding the rest. Simmer the mixture over a low heat for 5–7 minutes, stirring continuously to begin with to avoid lumps forming. If it becomes too thick, add more milk.

When your baby is a little older, you can try combining the flour with soy, nut or cow's milk. For variety, mix it with vegetable water or mashed vegetables; or, for a sweet dish, with fruit purées or juices.

Flaked millet, powdered oats and, later, semolina can all be used in a similar way. Once dairy products have been introduced, try adding a little grated cheese during cooking for a different taste.

Carrot Purée

Carrots are naturally sweet, rich in vitamins A, B, C and E; they also contain minerals, fibre and folic acid.

Scrape and chop the carrots, then cook in as little water as possible until mushy. Do not add salt. Drain and purée in a blender, freezing whatever is not immediately required in an ice tray.

For a change, mix the carrot purée with finely grated sweet apple, puréed potato or swede.

Mashed Potato

A useful early food, potatoes are full of potassium and vitamin C. They are filling, fibrous, versatile and easy to prepare. Potatoes mix well with all sorts of things a little later on: a dollop of yoghurt, Quark, fromage frais, cream cheese, grated cheese, smooth peanut butter, milk or puréed vegetables.

Peel, wash and dice the potatoes and cook in the smallest possible amount of boiling water without salt. Drain and purée with a little breast or formula milk, or combine with puréed carrot, leek or peas.

Leek Purée

Leeks have a surprisingly mild taste and a delightful pale green colour when puréed.

Use only the white parts of the leek, cutting off the green section and tough end. Make sure the leeks are thoroughly washed by slicing them lengthways and running them under the tap, taking great care to separate the leaves.

Slice up and cook in as little water as possible, without salt, until mushy and tender. Drain and purée with a little milk (breast or formula to start with), or mix with some cooked ground brown rice. Later on, this purée can be combined with other vegetables, cheese or yoghurt.

Cauliflower Purée

Despite its distinctive taste, many babies take to cauliflower especially when, after about 6 months, they can be introduced to dairy products and it can be combined with cheese.

Use only the florets at first, discarding the tough stems. Cook in a small amount of boiling water, without salt, until soft. Drain and purée with a little formula or breast milk if desired. If necessary, thin with a little of the vegetable cooking water. Once the baby can eat dairy products, mix the purée with some grated cheese or fromage frais.

Lentil Purée

Although some pulses may be a little heavy on the digestion in the early months, red lentils are easily assimilated and full of goodness. Unlike most other pulses, they do not need soaking (although it makes the cooking even easier if you leave them in cold water overnight), but make sure they are thoroughly washed. Lentils freeze well, so make enough to freeze in tiny quantities, in the ice tray.

Put the washed lentils in cold water and bring to the boil. Do not add salt. Turn down the heat and simmer for about 20–30 minutes (split lentils will cook faster than whole ones) until soft and breaking up. Add more water during cooking if necessary. Drain and purée in the blender.

For a change, use yellow split peas which have been washed and soaked overnight. When your baby has got used to lentils, you can begin cooking them with some chopped vegetables like carrots, potatoes or parsnips.

Once your baby has passed about 6 months and is establishing a recognizable eating pattern, you can start expanding your repertoire of foods, spending a little more time in their preparation and mixing things together to make meals more interesting. You may introduce mild cheese (in the light of knowledge about listeria poisoning, it is advised not to give soft cheeses to babies under a year old), natural yoghurt, soya products and different pulses and, from about 7 months, butter, wholemeal bread, wheat and oats.

Pear and Spinach Purée

Your baby's introduction to green vegetables must be pleasurable for, once recognized, they are impossible to disguise! Spinach can be very popular so long as you mask that bitter taste which can sometimes underlie it. This can be done by adding something which is naturally sweet, like a pear.

I suggest using frozen spinach balls or leaf spinach, so that you can defrost precisely what you need and no more. Simmer one such ball and a tiny knob of butter very gently over a low heat until defrosted and warmed through. Meanwhile, peel, core and slice up a small, very ripe, juicy pear and cook in a little boiling water until mushy. Drain, mash into the spinach with a fork, and serve warm.

Parsnip and Pear Purée

Another winning combination of fruit and vegetable is parsnip and pear. Parsnips provide vitamins A and C, fibre, potassium and calcium and are naturally sweet.

Peel a small parsnip and, for an infant with few if any teeth, take out the hard, fibrous middle. Dice it up and boil in the minimum amount of water until mushy. Meanwhile, cook the peeled and cored pear in a little boiling water until soft. Drain the parsnip and pear and blend together. Serve warm.

Spinach and Fromage Frais

Although spinach might not have quite as much iron in it as Popeye would have us believe, it does, nevertheless, contain valuable vitamins and minerals. In this combination, the bitter undertaste of the spinach is disguised by the creamy fromage frais.

Use frozen spinach balls or leaf spinach and defrost what you need over a low heat with a small knob of butter. Once it is warmed through, stir in a dollop of natural fromage frais. Warm through gently for a few seconds but do not boil.

Fromage frais is also good with puréed broccoli, courgette or marrow.

Broad Bean and Sweetcorn Purée

Most children take to the golden sweetness of sweetcorn, and the sooner they can eat it on the cob, the better. Until then, it can be puréed on its own or, for a change and for an added source of protein, calcium and iron, blended with broad beans. It is worth making enough of this to freeze, since I think this purée should be sieved to remove the tough skins of the beans.

Cook the frozen broad beans and sweetcorn together (in

about equal proportions) in a little boiling water until soft. Drain and purée. If the mixture seems too thick, add a little milk. Push the purée through a sieve. Reheat and serve, freezing what is not immediately required in convenient-sized containers.

Cottage Cheese and Sharon Fruit

Cottage cheese is delicious mixed with many fruits, and a good way of introducing baby to a few harmless lumps. It is especially good with Sharon fruit (persimmon) – a bright orange fruit which you may never have tried. Underneath its thick skin lies a sticky, sweet pulp – mash it up well with a little cottage cheese.

Another nutritious and tasty variation is cottage cheese and prunes. (Prunes should be rinsed, soaked overnight, and simmered in their soaking water for about 10 minutes, until soft. Watch out for stones.)

Sweet Potato and Orange

If you have not actually tasted sweet potatoes, they are as sweet as they sound and very appealing to young tastebuds.

Prepare sweet potatoes in the same way as ordinary ones: peel, boil in a little water, drain and then mash with a little butter. Add a dash of freshly squeezed orange juice; when baby has enough teeth, you can mix in peeled, chopped, orange segments (look out for pips).

Broccoli Cheese

Like all dark-green vegetables, broccoli is a good source of vitamins, important minerals and fibre.

Break the broccoli into small florets and cook in just enough boiling water to cover. When tender, drain. Add a dash of milk and grate a little cheese over the hot broccoli. Heat gently until the cheese has melted. Blend.

This is also good with cauliflower, leek or spinach.

Gradually, at your child's own pace, what he eats will begin to resemble what you think of as food! A few teeth will allow for the introduction of texture in the form of finger foods. Make sure the pieces of food are long enough to be easily grasped and thick enough not to break off too easily into bits which might choke him. Try wholemeal toast lightly spread with vegetable margarine or nutty spreads, peeled raw vegetables (carrots, celery, cucumber), cheese or peeled, pipped and cored fruit. His meals may now be mashed or chopped rather than puréed, but there is no need to rush if your baby still prefers smooth food for a while longer. Soon, you will be able to move on to more interesting recipes.

SOUPS

Soups, though difficult for children under about 18 months to manage on their own, are a wonderful food, especially during the cold autumn and winter months. The thick soups in this section, when served with wholemeal toast, bread or croutons, with perhaps some grated cheese on the side, make a complete meal.

Do experiment with the recipes, substituting your own choice of vegetables for the ones given here. Add pasta, brown rice or pot barley for extra bulk, and vary the consistency with a dash of cream, milk, or a dollop of plain yoghurt.

Although home-made stock is by no means essential, it really does improve both taste and nutritional content. You can make stock in reasonable quantities for freezing; it is not difficult and worth the effort. If you prefer to use stock cubes, try to buy from a health store those brands which are free from artificial additives and are either totally unsalted (eg Morga) or low in salt (eg Friggs).

Most of my soups have onions in them: these are extremely good for you, containing lots of vitamins and minerals. Disguised in soups, they add flavour and educate your baby's palate, yet are hardly discernible as a taste.

Basic Vegetable Stock

This is a simple way to make a basic stock and use up vegetables you have in the kitchen. It can be varied according to what you have to hand and combined with water in which you have cooked other vegetables (eg broccoli, marrow, carrot) if you wish.

1 onion, peeled and roughly quartered
1 stick celery, scrubbed and roughly chopped
1 leek, washed and roughly chopped
1 carrot, scrubbed and roughly chopped
a sprig of fresh or a pinch of dried herbs (rosemary,
    dill, fennel, thyme)
a bay leaf

Put all the prepared vegetables with the herbs in a saucepan and cover generously with cold water (about $1\frac{1}{2}$ pts). Bring to the boil, cover and bubble vigorously for about 20 minutes, adding more water if necessary. Strain immediately, then use, or cool and freeze.

Pumpkin Soup

Pumpkins are perfect for making thick, richly autumnal soups.

675 g / $1\frac{1}{2}$ lb pumpkin, peeled, seeds removed and
    diced
1 large carrot, scraped and diced
1 medium potato, peeled and diced
25 g / 1 oz butter or margarine
$\frac{1}{4}$ pt milk
$\frac{1}{4}$ pt home-made vegetable stock (see p. 22), or $\frac{1}{2}$
    unsalted vegetable stock cube dissolved in boil-
    ing water
a bay leaf
single cream or plain yoghurt (optional)
wholemeal croutons

Melt the butter or margarine in a large heavy-bottomed saucepan. Stir in all the prepared vegetables and simmer gently for about 5 minutes, stirring occasionally to prevent burning or sticking. Do not let them brown.

Stir in the stock, milk and bay leaf and simmer for about 20 minutes or until the vegetables are tender. Cool slightly, remove the bay leaf, and put through the blender. Return to the cooker and heat through gently before serving.

To make this a real meal, serve with a dollop of single cream or natural yoghurt on the top and a scattering of croutons. These are simply cubes of wholemeal bread fried until crisp and brown in vegetable oil. Drain on kitchen roll before adding to the soup, and let your child stir them in!

Cream of Sweetcorn Soup

An absolute winner, this soup is golden, creamy and surprisingly filling.

450 g/1 lb frozen sweetcorn
1 small onion, finely chopped
25 g/1 oz of butter or margarine
25 g/1 oz wholemeal flour
$\frac{1}{2}$ pt milk
$\frac{1}{2}$ pt home-made vegetable stock (see p. 22), or $\frac{1}{2}$ unsalted vegetable stock cube dissolved in boiling water

Melt the butter or margarine in a heavy-bottomed saucepan. Add the onion and cook gently for about 5 minutes until transparent, stirring to prevent sticking. Do not let it brown.

Blend in the flour and cook gently, stirring continuously, for a few minutes. Gradually stir in the milk and the stock, then add the frozen sweetcorn. Bring to the boil, stirring.

Turn down the heat and simmer gently for about 25 minutes. Cool slightly, then purée. Reheat and serve.

Carrot and Apple Soup

Like my pumpkin soup, this is thick, colourful and naturally sweet. The addition of barley gives it body and extra goodness in the form of protein and valuable minerals like iron, calcium and potassium. Choose 'pot' rather than pearl barley which has had its outer layers and thereby most of the goodness removed.

450 g / 1 lb carrots, scraped and diced
1 small onion, finely chopped
1 medium potato, peeled and diced
1 large eating apple, peeled, cored and roughly chopped
25 g / 1 oz butter or margarine
25 g / 1 oz pot barley, rinsed in cold water
2 pts home-made vegetable stock (see p. 22), or 1 unsalted vegetable stock cube dissolved in boiling water
1 tsp yeast extract
1 dsp tomato purée

Melt the butter or margarine in a heavy-bottomed saucepan. Stir in the carrots, onion and potato and cook gently for a few minutes, stirring to prevent sticking or browning. Stir in the apple, stock, yeast extract and tomato purée. Bring to the boil and add the pot barley. Stir, reduce the heat to a simmer, cover and cook for about 45 minutes – 1 hour, or until the barley is tender (it should not be chewy).

Remove from the heat, allow to cool a little, then blend. Reheat before serving.

This is another soup which tastes great with wholemeal croutons – fry cubes of wholemeal bread in hot oil until crisp and brown. Serve them in a bowl and let the children float their own on top! The soup freezes well if you have any left over.

Parsnip Chowder

Parsnips have a very distinctive taste which you either like or you don't. If you do, this soup has a lovely creamy colour and texture, and can be frozen for later use.

450 g/1 lb parsnips, peeled and diced
450 g/1 lb potatoes, peeled and diced
1 small onion, finely chopped
25 g/ 1 oz margarine or butter
$1\frac{1}{2}$ pts home-made vegetable stock (see p. 22), or 1 unsalted vegetable stock cube dissolved in boiling water
a bay leaf
a pinch of dried or freshly chopped parsley or dill

Melt the margarine or butter in a heavy-bottomed saucepan. Add the onion and fry gently for about 3 minutes until transparent, stirring to prevent sticking or browning. Add the potatoes and parsnips and cook for a further few minutes, stirring occasionally. Stir in the stock, bay leaf and herbs and bring to the boil.

Reduce the heat to a simmer, cover and cook for about 25–30 minutes until the vegetables are tender and beginning to fall apart. Remove the bay leaf, cool slightly and blend. Reheat gently before serving, adding a little more stock, water or milk if the soup is too thick.

Lentil and Tomato Soup

This is a thick, nourishing and tasty soup which, if served with brown bread, a warm wholewheat chapati or pitta bread, provides a meal rich in complete protein. The beauty of lentils is that they require no soaking.

100 g/4 oz red lentils, washed
$\frac{1}{2}$ × 400 g/14 oz tin Italian peeled plum tomatoes,
    chopped up with their juice
1 carrot, scraped and chopped
1 small onion, finely chopped
1 tbsp pure vegetable oil
1 pt water
a pinch of dried or freshly chopped parsley, dill or
    thyme
1 dsp single cream or top-of-the-milk

Thoroughly rinse the lentils in several changes of cold water. Heat the oil in a heavy saucepan. Add the onion and cook gently for about 3 minutes until transparent, stirring to prevent burning or sticking. Stir in the carrot and cook for a further few minutes, before adding the water and lentils. Bring to the boil and bubble for several minutes skimming off any scum from the top with a spoon. Reduce the heat and add the tomatoes.

Cover and simmer gently for 30 minutes to an hour or until the lentils are completely soft and breaking up. (Split lentils will take less time than whole ones.) Thin down with more boiling water during cooking if the soup is becoming too thick.

Take off the heat, cool slightly and blend. Reheat gently and stir in a little top-of-the-milk or cream before serving if desired. Serve with wholemeal bread and grated cheese.

Potato and Leek

This is a variation on the traditional Vichysoisse and has a lovely light colour and taste. I prefer to make soups thicker rather than thinner, since a watery soup is more trouble than it is worth with a sloppy eater!

450 g/1 lb leeks, the white part, washed and thinly
  sliced
450 g/1 lb potatoes, peeled and diced
1 small onion, finely chopped
25 g/1 oz margarine or butter
1½ pts home-made vegetable stock (see p. 22), or 1
  unsalted vegetable stock cube dissolved in boiling water
a bay leaf
a pinch of freshly chopped or dried parsley

Melt the margarine or butter in a heavy saucepan. Add the
onion, leeks and potatoes and cook gently for about 5 minutes,
stirring regularly to prevent sticking or browning. Pour in the
stock and add the parsley and bay leaf. Bring to the boil.

Turn down the heat, cover and simmer for about 30 minutes
until the vegetables are soft and the potatoes beginning to fall
apart. Cool slightly, remove the bay leaf and put through the
blender. If the soup needs thinning down, add a little milk.

Serve warm with wholemeal toast, muffin or crumpet.

Split Pea Soup

A classic winter warmer with a deep yellow colour and rich,
earthy taste.

100–175 g/4–6 oz dried split peas, rinsed and
  soaked overnight
50 g/2 oz butter or margarine
1 small onion, finely chopped
1 small clove garlic, crushed
1 large carrot, scraped and diced
1 stick celery, scrubbed and chopped (or 1 leek, the
  white part, washed and sliced)

1 medium potato, peeled and diced
1 tsp yeast extract
$1\frac{1}{2}$ pts home-made vegetable stock (see p. 22), or 1
    unsalted vegetable stock cube dissolved in boil-
    ing water
a bay leaf

Rinse the split peas in several changes of water then soak in fresh cold water overnight. Drain, retaining the soaking water.

Melt the butter or margarine in a heavy saucepan and add all the prepared vegetables. Cook gently for about 5 minutes, stirring to prevent sticking.

Using the water in which the peas were soaked and the vegetable stock, make up 2 pints of liquid. Add this to the vegetables with the split peas, yeast extract and bay leaf. Bring to the boil and remove any scum from the top with a spoon. Reduce the heat, cover and simmer for an hour or so, until the split peas are soft and falling apart. (It is difficult to be precise about the time required to cook pulses since it depends on their age, type and the length of time they have been soaked.)

Cool slightly, remove the bay leaf, and put through the blender. Serve with wholemeal toast or croutons.

Winter Vegetable Soup

For this soup, you can put together whatever vegetables you have to hand, with potatoes, carrots, onions and leeks providing the backbone of the recipe.

675–900 g / $1\frac{1}{2}$–2 lbs mixed winter vegetables, which
    may include all or some of the following:
1 large carrot, scrubbed and chopped
1 large potato, peeled and diced
1 small turnip, peeled and diced

$\frac{1}{4}$ medium swede, peeled and diced
1 leek, the white part, washed and chopped
1 stick celery, washed and chopped
1 small parsnip, peeled and diced
1 small onion, finely chopped
2 pts home-made vegetable stock (see p.22), or 1
  unsalted vegetable stock cube dissolved in boiling water
1 tbsp pure vegetable oil
1 tsp yeast extract
1 dsp tomato purée
a bay leaf
a pinch of mixed herbs

Heat the oil in a heavy saucepan. Add all the prepared veg-etables and cook gently, stirring frequently to avoid browning or sticking, for about 5 minutes.

Add the stock, herbs, tomato purée, yeast extract and bay leaf and bring to the boil. Turn down the heat, cover and simmer for 25–30 minutes until all the vegetables are soft.

Cool slightly, remove the bay leaf and blend. Serve with grated cheese on top and a wholemeal bap or roll.

MAIN MEALS:
PULSE, PASTA, GRAIN AND VEGETABLE

The key to cooking PULSES is to allow sufficient soaking time, and not to add salt until the end as this retards the softening process.

All pulses should be thoroughly washed and any discoloured beans or small stones removed, then left to soak overnight in clean cold water – cover generously because they will expand. The only varieties which do not require soaking are lentils, yellow split peas and aduki beans.

Pulses should generally be cooked in the water they have been soaked in, for as long as it takes for them to become soft all the way through. Bring them to the boil and remove any scum from the surface before reducing the heat to a simmer. Red kidney beans *must* be boiled vigorously for at least 10 minutes to destroy a poisonous substance in this bean. The cooking time required for pulses will vary enormously depending on their age, type and how long they have been stored.

The nutrients in VEGETABLES can be damaged by heat, light and poor storage conditions, so how can we best retain all the goodness within them?

Select the best by feeling them. Buy only those which are fresh and firm, and discard those which are limp, discoloured, soggy or bruised. Store them in a dark, cool place rather than an open vegetable rack.

In most vegetables and fruit, much of the goodness is concentrated just below the surface of the skin so, whenever possible, avoid peeling – simply wash and scrub.

Vegetables are best prepared in a way which facilitates fast cooking by exposing the greatest possible surface area to the heat. Rather than cutting root vegetables into large chunks, for example, slice carrots diagonally in long strips. This technique applies particularly to stir-frying and steaming when, if the vegetables are not thinly sliced, the outside is cooked while the inside is hard.

Overcooking leads to mushy, tasteless vegetables whose valuable nutrients have all disappeared into the cooking water. So, cook vegetables in the minimum amount of boiling water for the least possible time. And do not leave vegetables to soak, either before or after cooking.

Before the main recipes, here are a couple of useful tips. First, a quick method for a tomato sauce which is a useful accompaniment for some of the meals below. I have found that my son goes through 'wet' and 'dry' food phases – at one point, he would not eat anything like patties, fritters, rissoles etc. which did not have a sauce over them. Later, he went off moist-looking foods for a while and suddenly liked things which had been crispened and browned, and wanted all his foods distinctly separate on the plate.

Quick Tomato Sauce

Tinned tomatoes are a useful ingredient for many sauces and recipes. They also provide the basis for a simple sauce, which can be made less tomatoey if required with natural yoghurt or top-of-the-milk.

about $\frac{1}{3}$ × 400 g/14 oz tin Italian peeled plum
  tomatoes with their juice
dollop of natural yoghurt, or dash of top-of-the-
  milk, or single cream
cornflour for thickening (optional)

Purée the tomatoes in some of their juice and heat up. Mix with a little natural yoghurt, milk, or cream and heat gently – do not boil. If you wish to make the sauce thicker, add a little cornflour (do not forget to follow packet instructions, first mixing it with cold water into a paste, otherwise the sauce will go lumpy).

My second tip is for breadcrumbs, which I use in a number of recipes.

Wholemeal Breadcrumbs

Save up bits of wholemeal bread and crusts over three or four days, then break them up and put them through a food processor, blender or coffee grinder until you have fine breadcrumbs. The breadcrumbs can be frozen in small bags containing a few ounces each for use as needed. It is easier to make large quantities since food processors sometimes find it difficult to cope properly with one or two slices of bread and coffee grinders can be a fiddle to clean (the best way of cleaning the grinder, incidentally, is to whizz some dry bread around in it). I do recommend using your own breadcrumbs – they taste quite different to dried packaged ones.

Lentil and Raisin Cakes

Pulses are an indispensable source of protein, iron and B vitamins; they are tasty, versatile and easy to prepare, especially lentils which need no prior soaking. Where possible, serve with a grain such as rice to give a meal rich in complete protein.

100 g/4 oz red lentils, washed
1 small onion, finely chopped

25 g / 1 oz raisins
$\frac{1}{2}$ tbsp tomato purée
1 free-range egg, beaten
a dash of lemon juice
a pinch of parsley, freshly chopped or dried
fresh wholemeal breadcrumbs
pure vegetable oil for shallow frying

Rinse the lentils in several changes of cold water. Bring them to the boil in about three times as much fresh water, then reduce the heat and simmer for about 30 minutes, or until tender. (It is difficult to be precise about cooking time since this varies with age and type, so always taste.) Meanwhile, fry the onion gently in a little oil until tender and transparent.

When the lentils are cooked, drain off the excess cooking water. Stir the onions, raisins, parsley, lemon juice and tomato purée into the lentils. Cook gently for a further 10 minutes, stirring occasionally. Allow the mixture to cool, then chill in the fridge for 30 minutes.

Divide and shape into flat little cakes. Dip these first into the beaten egg and then coat in breadcrumbs. Heat enough oil to cover the bottom of a frying pan. Fry the cakes for about 8 minutes turning once, until golden. Drain on kitchen roll. Serve warm with brown rice and a fresh vegetable.

Butterbean Stew

Beans are one of the healthiest foods in the world, and butter beans amongst the most delicate of all. Do not let the idea of having to soak beans put you off: just give them a good rinse and leave them overnight covered in cold water. If you are really in a hurry, you may soak the beans for an hour in boiling water and then cook, although I still prefer overnight soaking. Allow yourself time to cook beans properly; undercooked, they taste horrible and are quite indigestible. I often add a pinch of caraway seeds to cooking pulses as this seems to reduce the flatulence they are renowned for producing! However, some sources suggest that the more beans you eat, the less of a problem this becomes.

Bean dishes freeze very well so you can decide whether you want to multiply the quantities for this purpose.

> 100 g/4 oz butter beans (or haricot beans), washed and soaked overnight
> 2 carrots, scraped and diced
> 1 small onion, finely chopped
> 2 medium potatoes, peeled and diced
> 1 leek, the white part, chopped
> 1 pt home-made vegetable stock (see p. 22), or 1 unsalted vegetable stock cube dissolved in boiling water
> 1 tbsp tomato purée
> 1 tbsp olive or other pure vegetable oil
> 1 tsp tahini (sesame paste)
> a bay leaf
> a pinch of dried herbs (parsley, oregano, thyme)

Cook the butter beans in the water they were soaked in, adding more fresh water if necessary. Bring to the boil, then simmer for about 20 minutes. Drain, retaining the water. Combine this water with the stock to make up about $1\frac{1}{2}$ pints of liquid.

Heat enough oil to just cover the bottom of a heavy saucepan. Fry the onion for a few minutes, then add the other vegetables and cook for a further 5 minutes, stirring occasionally to prevent sticking or burning.

Add the partly cooked beans, the stock, tomato purée, tahini, herbs and bay leaf. Bring to the boil, then turn down, cover and simmer until the beans are soft but not falling apart. (During cooking, thin down with boiling water, more stock or milk, if required.)

Serve hot with brown rice, or bulghur wheat. Any leftovers can be liquidized to give a thick, creamy soup.

Pease Pudding

A traditional British dish, pease pudding is simple to make and, served with brown rice or bulghur wheat, makes a hearty, warming winter meal. Leftovers may be frozen, or thinned down with milk and/or stock to give a thick yellow soup.

100 g/4 oz yellow split peas, washed and soaked
   overnight
$\frac{1}{2}$ small onion, cut in half
1 small parsnip, peeled and roughly sliced
1 carrot, peeled and roughly sliced
sprigs of fresh parsley and thyme
1 pt water
25 g/1 oz butter or margarine

Rinse the peas in several changes of cold water, cover with fresh water and soak overnight.

Using the water in which the peas were soaked, make up to 1 pint with fresh water. Put this in a saucepan with the peas, onion, carrot, parsnip and herbs. (All the vegetables will be removed later so do not chop finely.) Bring to the boil, then lower the heat and simmer for about 45 minutes or until the peas are mushy and very tender.

Drain off the water and remove the vegetables and herbs, leaving the peas in the pan. Add the butter or margarine and beat into a soft purée with a wooden spoon. Serve hot with brown rice or wholemeal bread.

Bean Pie

Almost any kind or combination of beans can be used here, although red and black kidney beans might be a little too heavy for toddlers.

100 g/4 oz haricot/pinto/black-eyed beans, washed and soaked overnight
1 small onion, finely chopped
1 large carrot, scraped and sliced thinly
1 × 400 g/14 oz tin Italian peeled plum tomatoes, mashed with their own juice
225–275 g/8–10 oz potatoes, peeled, cooked and mashed
2 sticks celery, scrubbed and chopped
1 tsp yeast extract
a pinch of dried herbs (parsley, thyme, oregano, basil)
1 tbsp olive or other pure vegetable oil

Rinse the beans in several changes of cold water. Cover with fresh water and soak overnight. Bring the beans to the boil in the soaking water, adding more boiling water if necessary. Simmer for as long as it takes to make them tender all the way through (at least an hour or so, probably longer – pulses vary enormously depending on their age and type). Drain, reserving the cooking liquid.

Heat the oil in a saucepan and gently fry the onion until soft. Add the carrots and celery and fry for a few minutes before adding the tomatoes, herbs and cooked beans. Pour in the bean cooking liquid, add the yeast extract and bring to the boil. Meanwhile, cook and mash the potatoes.

When the bean stew is ready, put it into a small, deep casserole dish, cover it with mashed potato, dot with butter and brown under a hot grill. Serve hot with wholemeal bread.

Kidney Bean Casserole

Very young children might find kidney beans a little heavy, but by about two years old they seem to be ready for them. I thought they were unsuitable until my son started picking them out of a salad I was eating … now he eats this winter dish with relish. Kidney beans are rich in protein, high in iron and vitamin A; they also actually reduce the cholesterol in the bloodstream. Married with grain, you have a perfect, protein-filled meal. But do remember that this is the pulse you need to boil – the toxin in it requires 10 vigorous minutes to destroy it!

I like to make this in quantities large enough to freeze – this recipe can feed about six children. You can, of course, vary this dish by using other beans or pulses, eg pinto, black-eyed or haricot beans.

> 225 g/8 oz red kidney beans, washed, soaked over-
> night and cooked
> 100 g/4 oz carrots, scraped and sliced
> 2 celery stalks, scrubbed and sliced
> 1 medium potato, peeled and diced
> 1 leek, the white part, washed and sliced
> 1 small onion, finely chopped
> 1 clove garlic, crushed
> 1 pt vegetable stock (make this up with the liquid
> the beans were cooked in combined with $\frac{1}{2}$ un-
> salted stock cube dissolved in boiling water)
> $\frac{1}{3}$ pt milk
> 2 tbsp pure vegetable oil
> 1 tsp yeast extract
> 1 tbsp tomato purée

Rinse the beans in several changes of cold water then leave to soak overnight in fresh water. Drain the beans, cover with more fresh water and boil briskly for 10 minutes.

Turn down the heat and simmer until tender but not mushy (this can take anything from 45 minutes–2 hours depending on their age and type). Drain, reserving the liquid for the stock.

Heat the oil in a heavy saucepan and add all the prepared vegetables. Cook them over a medium heat for about 5 minutes, stirring occasionally to prevent burning. Add the cooked kidney beans, the stock, the milk, tomato purée and yeast extract. Mix well together and bring to the boil. Reduce the heat and simmer gently for 30 minutes.

Serve with brown rice or bulghur wheat. This casserole keeps well in the fridge and loses nothing in the re-heating. If you would like to do something different with leftovers, try using the beans as a filling for a Mexican 'taco' (see p. 62).

Mushroom Pasticcio

For this recipe, you may use any small wholewheat pasta shapes you have in the house: macaroni, pasta bows, small shells or twists. Like many casserole pasta dishes, this can be made ahead of time and baked later. You may also wish to try using a different vegetable – courgette works well.

100 g/4 oz small wholewheat pasta bows
100 g/4 oz fresh button mushrooms, wiped and sliced
1 free-range egg, beaten
4 fl. oz milk
25 g/1 oz Cheddar, or other hard cheese, grated
10 g/$\frac{1}{2}$ oz butter or margarine
10 g/$\frac{1}{2}$ oz wholemeal flour
fresh wholemeal breadcrumbs

Preheat the oven to GM5/375°F/190°C.

Melt the butter or margarine in a small frying pan and cook the mushrooms on a medium heat for about 5 minutes, stirring occasionally. Remove from the pan and put aside. Boil the pasta until tender but not soggy. Drain.

In a bowl, mix together the egg, milk and flour. Stir in the mushrooms. Fold the mixture carefully into the cooked pasta and pour into a non-stick casserole dish. Top with breadcrumbs and grated cheese and cook in the oven until brown and set (approx. 15–20 minutes).

Cheese Noodles

Wholewheat noodles are a useful ingredient in your storecupboard since they only take 4 minutes to cook! They are very versatile and can be used in a variety of ways – here is one of them.

75–100 g/3–4 oz of wholewheat noodles
50 g/2 oz Ricotta, curd or cottage cheese
25 g/1 oz margarine or butter
25 g/1 oz wholemeal flour
$\frac{1}{4}$–$\frac{1}{2}$ pt milk
1 dsp tomato purée

Cook the noodles in boiling water until tender but not soggy. Melt the margarine or butter in a medium saucepan and blend in the flour over a low heat. Cook gently for a few minutes, stirring. Slowly add about $\frac{1}{4}$ pint milk, stirring constantly. Bring to the boil, then lower the heat and stir in the cheese and tomato purée. Simmer for a few minutes, and add more milk if the sauce seems too thick.

Fold in the cooked noodles, holding some back if the dish seems to be getting too dry. Heat through and serve warm.

Tagliatelle Bolognese

Lentils, perhaps unexpectedly, combine well with pasta, and this recipe resembles a meatless bolognese. You can use any kind of ribbon pasta or spaghetti.

Although lentils are the quickest cooking of the pulses, do not underestimate how long they take: on a slow simmer, whole lentils might take up to an hour to be really mushy and soft. (Split lentils will take considerably less time.)

> 75 g/3 oz red lentils, washed
> 75 g/3 oz wholewheat tagliatelle or spaghetti
> 1 carrot, scraped and chopped
> $\frac{1}{2}$ small onion, finely chopped
> 1 clove garlic, crushed
> $\frac{1}{2}$ × 400 g/14 oz tin Italian peeled plum tomatoes, drained and chopped
> $\frac{1}{2}-\frac{3}{4}$ pt water or vegetable stock (see p. 22)
> $\frac{1}{2}$ tsp yeast extract
> 1 dsp olive oil
> a pinch of dried herbs (parsley, oregano, sweet basil)
> 2 dsps natural yoghurt

Thoroughly rinse the lentils in several changes of cold water. Heat the oil in a saucepan and gently fry the onion, carrot and garlic until the vegetables are softened (about 5 minutes). Stir to prevent sticking and browning.

Add the tomatoes, water or stock, and lentils. Bring to the boil. Reduce the heat and add the herbs and yeast extract. Simmer for about 45 minutes or until the lentils are soft and mushy. When the lentils are almost ready, cook the pasta *al dente* (tender but not soggy). Drain the pasta and fold carefully into the lentils. Gently stir in the yoghurt and simmer on a low heat for a further few minutes. Serve hot.

Vegetable Pilaff

Rice is a perfect food for children − filling, easily digestible and nutritious. Unless you are serving fish in the meal, I would make a point of preferring brown rice which has all the goodness of the whole grain left in it.

> 100 g/4 oz brown rice, washed
> 50 g/2 oz button mushrooms, wiped and sliced
> 50 g/2 oz frozen sweetcorn
> 35 g/1$\frac{1}{2}$ oz butter or margarine
> $\frac{1}{2}$ small onion, finely chopped
> 1 clove garlic, crushed
> 1 large carrot, scraped and finely chopped (alternatively, use the white part of a leek, or a stick of celery, finely chopped)
> 25 g/1 oz raisins
> $\frac{1}{2}$ pt home-made vegetable stock (see p. 22), or $\frac{1}{2}$ unsalted vegetable stock cube dissolved in boiling water

Preheat the oven to GM4/350°F/180°C. Wash the rice in several changes of cold water.

Melt the butter in a medium saucepan and gently fry the onion, garlic and carrot until softened (about 5 minutes), stirring to prevent burning. Stir in the rice and cook for a further 5 minutes, stirring occasionally. Add the mushrooms, frozen sweetcorn and stock. Bring to the boil, then transfer to a small casserole dish. Cover and cook in the oven for 35 minutes.

Stir in the raisins. (If the rice is not yet tender but looks too dry, add a little boiling water, checking first with a knife that there is no water left at the bottom of the dish.) Replace the lid and cook for another 10 minutes until all the liquid is absorbed and the rice is fluffy and cooked. Serve hot.

Egg and Spinach Rice

We all know how good spinach is for us but many parents are afraid to give it to their children – they fear that it will be rejected. My son loves it and I think that the trick is to cook it with something which takes away that slightly sharp aftertaste which spinach can have. Fresh young spinach is always the most delicious, but frozen is perfectly acceptable. Use the balls or leaf spinach rather than the solid blocks, since these are impossible to cut sections off.

> 100 g/4 oz brown rice, washed
> 100 g/4 oz spinach, fresh or frozen
> 1 tsp sesame seeds
> 1 free-range egg, beaten
> 25 g/1 oz butter

Rinse the rice in several changes of cold water. Cover, in a saucepan, with about twice its volume of fresh water and bring to the boil. Stir, reduce the heat to a simmer, cover with a lid and cook gently until all the water is absorbed and the rice is fluffy and tender. If the rice starts to dry out before it is properly cooked, add a little more boiling water. Let the rice cool down.

Gently melt the butter in a large frying pan. Add the sesame seeds and fry for a few minutes, stirring continuously. Add the spinach. (If fresh, wash, remove stalks and central stems, and shred roughly.) Gently cook over a low heat until the frozen spinach is defrosted, or the fresh spinach wilted. Stir occasionally to prevent burning. Carefully mix in the cooked rice.

Turn the heat up a little and pour the beaten egg over the top of the spinach rice. Leave for a minute or so, then, stirring frequently, allow the egg to cook through. It will look like a mushy mess to begin with until the egg starts to set! Serve hot.

Vegetable Fried Rice

This adaptation of traditional Chinese fried rice must use cold, cooked white rice or it will go sticky. For this reason, it is a marvellous way to use up leftover rice from a previous meal. So, if you are cooking rice one evening, do more than you need and try this recipe for lunch next day. White rice provides an occasional change from brown rice and, provided it is combined with protein (for example, fish, egg or tofu), makes a substantial meal. I include a few exotic vegetables in this recipe, but you can basically use what you want – try tomatoes, sweetcorn, courgettes, broccoli, or cauliflower.

To cook white rice, rinse it several times in cold water then bring to the boil in about twice its volume of fresh water. Stir it once, cover and simmer until all the water is absorbed. If in doubt, use less rather than more water and simply add more boiling water during cooking if necessary. You should then have perfect fluffy rice.

The quantities of vegetables used here are simply a guide – you just need a little of each.

100 g/4 oz cold, cooked white rice
a few tinned bamboo shoots or water chestnuts, chopped (the remainder should be kept in the fridge in their juice and used up in stir-fry dishes)
a handful of beansprouts or alfalfa sprouts
1 carrot, scraped and finely sliced lengthways
2 spring onions, finely chopped
25–50 g/1–2 oz button mushrooms, wiped and finely sliced
25 g/1 oz of frozen peas (run under a warm tap for a moment to defrost)
1 free-range egg, beaten (or some diced tofu, or beancurd)
$\frac{1}{2}$ tsp unrefined brown cane sugar

1 dsp soy sauce
$1\frac{1}{2}$ tbsps pure vegetable oil (sesame is delicious for stir-frying)

Prepare all your vegetables before you start. Heat $\frac{1}{2}$ tbsp oil in a wok or large frying pan and cook the spring onions over a medium heat for about 2−3 minutes, stirring to prevent browning. Add the beaten egg if used. When it looks about to set, mix it gently, scrambling lightly. Fluff the rice up with your fingers and sprinkle it into the pan. Mix carefully with the onion and egg and cook for 2 minutes.

Now take the mixture out of the pan and keep aside. Heat up 1 tablespoon oil, and add the carrots (and any other firm vegetables). Cook for 2 minutes, stirring continuously. Add all the other vegetables, except the beansprouts, and the tofu, if used. Stir fry for about 3 minutes, then add the beansprouts. Stir fry for a further minute, then add the soy sauce and sugar. Stir for a minute. Return the rice mixture to the pan, mixing it in gently. Heat through and serve.

Spinach and Cheese Pancakes

My son and I love pancakes but, I have to admit, my attempts are rarely totally successful. But I have now found the foolproof method − I buy a packet of 'Brittany Pancakes'! They contain only pure ingredients and are completely authentic; although they are sold in packets of 10, I never have any trouble using them up. They keep well in the fridge for several days, so you can eat them for breakfast with eggs, mushrooms and cheese inside or use up spares for dessert with lemon juice, fruit and yoghurt. Most good supermarkets stock them − if not, keep your eyes open in delicatessens.

For those of you brave enough to make your own, I include a recipe for pancakes too (see p. 47).

2 Brittany pancakes (or several home-made buckwheat pancakes, see below)
6–8 frozen spinach balls/mini portions (buy in
450 g/1 lb pkt)
25 g/1 oz butter or margarine
25 g/1 oz wholemeal flour
50 g/2 oz grated cheese
about 7 fl. oz milk

Defrost the spinach very gently over a low heat, stirring frequently to prevent burning.

In a medium saucepan, gently melt the butter and blend in
the flour. Cook over a low heat for a few minutes, stirring.
Gradually add the milk and bring to the boil, stirring constantly.
Add the cheese. Reduce the heat and simmer for a few minutes.
(The sauce should not be too runny.) Stir in the spinach and
remove from the heat.

Heat the oven to GM6/400°F/200°C. Unfold the Brittany pancakes once (or lay out the home-made ones) so that you are
using them with double thickness. Moisten with a little milk.

Put some sauce across the pancake near one of the edges,
then roll up. Lay in an ovenproof dish and put in the oven for
2–4 minutes until the pancakes and filling are hot. Do not let
the pancakes crispen. Serve.

Buckwheat Pancakes

50 g/2 oz buckwheat flour
50 g/2 oz wholemeal flour
1 free-range egg
$\frac{1}{2}$ pt milk
tiny pinch salt
1 tbsp pure vegetable oil
vegetable oil for frying

Put the flours and salt into a mixing bowl and make a well in the centre. Break the egg into the well and pour in a little less than half of the milk. Using a wooden spoon, mix the ingredients together by gradually drawing in the flour from around the edge of the bowl. When all the flour has been mixed in, add the remaining milk and the oil, beating well to give a smooth batter. Leave it to stand for 30 minutes.

Pancakes are best made in a pancake or omelette pan (6–8″ diameter) but, failing that, use a frying pan which is not going to stick.

Heat the pan and put in just enough oil to grease the pan thoroughly. Pour 2–3 tablespoons of batter into the pan, then quickly tilt it from side to side in order to coat the bottom evenly. Cook the pancake until its underside is golden brown. Turn and cook the other side. Repeat the procedure for each pancake, keeping the cooked ones warm in a stack in the oven.

There are many possible fillings for savoury pancakes. Try broccoli and mushrooms in a cheese sauce; or flaked white fish or prawns and chopped egg in a cheese sauce; or a fried egg with grated cheese.

Cauliflower Cheese

This good old standard is still one of the few ways children seem to like cauliflower. It is surprisingly high in vitamin C and supplies good amounts of other vitamins and minerals too. The latter are particularly abundant in the tender pale green leaves, so do leave some on. Also make sure that you buy fresh cauliflower; as with so many vegetables, frozen cauliflower loses much of its goodness.

When cooking vegetables in water, use as little as possible and, if you are making a sauce using stock, keep the cooking water to add to it. Otherwise you lose those nutrients which have seeped into the water. (Steaming minimizes this, of course.)

1 small cauliflower, or part of a large one
$\frac{1}{2}$ pt liquid made up from $\frac{1}{4}$ pt of cauliflower cooking
  water and $\frac{1}{4}$ pt milk
75 g/3 oz Cheddar, or other hard cheese, grated
25 g/1 oz wholemeal flour
25 g/1 oz butter or margarine
$\frac{1}{2}$ tsp Dijon mustard (optional)

Trim the cauliflower and break into small florets. Cook in enough water to cover, until tender but not soggy. Drain, keeping aside the water. With milk make up this liquid to $\frac{1}{2}$ pint.

Gently melt the butter or margarine in a medium saucepan and blend in the flour. Cook over a low heat, stirring frequently, for a few minutes. Gradually add the milk/water and, stirring continuously, bring to the boil. Cook for a few minutes, then reduce the heat and stir in the cheese, and mustard if required. Simmer for a further few minutes. Fold in the cauliflower florets. Heat through and serve, either on its own or on brown rice.

Sweetcorn Fritters

This recipe can usefully be adapted for other vegetables. Buckwheat flour, which is speckled and tastes slightly nutty, makes a wonderful change from other flours and is excellent for fritters. You can find it in most health food shops.

$\frac{1}{2}$ × 400 g/14 oz tin American- or Canadian-style
  creamed sweetcorn
50 g/2 oz buckwheat flour
1 free-range egg
1 tbsp pure vegetable oil

Sift the flour into a mixing bowl. Make a well in the centre and break the egg into it. Using a wooden spoon, mix in the egg, gradually drawing in the flour around the edges. Beat well. Stir in the sweetcorn.

Heat the oil in a frying pan until very hot but not smoking. Carefully drop tablespoonfuls of the mixture into the oil, turn down the heat a little, and cook until lightly browned on both sides. Drain on kitchen roll. Serve hot with mashed potato and a fresh vegetable.

Cauliflower Fritters

This is a good variation on the sweetcorn recipe given above and is prepared in a similar way.

$\frac{1}{2}$ small cauliflower
50 g/2 oz buckwheat flour
1 free-range egg
50 g/2 oz Cheddar, or other hard cheese, grated
1 tbsp pure vegetable oil

Break the cauliflower into florets and cook in a little boiling water until tender. Drain, cool and chop finely.

Sift the flour into a mixing bowl and make a well in the centre. Break the egg into the well and gradually, using a wooden spoon, draw in the flour from around the edges. Beat well. Mix in the cauliflower and the cheese.

Heat the oil in a frying pan until very hot but not smoking, then carefully drop in tablespoons of the mixture. Reduce the heat a little, and fry until golden on both sides. Drain on kitchen roll. Serve hot with mashed potato.

Cheesy Leek and Potatoes

You can try this recipe with carrots or courgettes as well as leeks.

450 g/1 lb potatoes (if new, scrub and leave the skins on)

1 large leek, the white part, washed and thinly sliced

1 free-range egg, beaten

$\frac{1}{2}$ pt milk

50–75 g/2–3 oz Cheddar, or other hard cheese, grated

Preheat the oven to GM5/375°F/190°C.

Peel and boil the potatoes for about 10 minutes, until tender but still firm (there should still be a little resistance to the fork). Wash, trim and thinly slice the leeks. Cook in a little boiling water until tender.

Let the potatoes cool a little, then slice them thinly. Lay them and the leeks in overlapping layers on the bottom of a shallow ovenproof dish. Mix the beaten egg with the milk and most of the cheese (leaving a little for the top) and pour over the layers. Top with the remaining grated cheese. Put in the oven until lightly set and browned (30–40 minutes). Serve hot.

Chinese Stir-fry

The tofu (soya beancurd) used in this recipe is a marvellous source of concentrated protein. Being rather bland, it absorbs the flavour of whatever it is cooked with and can therefore be used in either savoury or sweet dishes. It is easily digestible and supplies all sorts of nutrients, amongst them calcium and iron. Tofu is usually sold in vacuum-sealed blocks; what is not immediately used can be kept in the fridge for about a week, so long as it is covered with water (this should be changed daily). Before use, rinse the tofu taken from the packet in cold water.

Remember, the trick of a stir-fry is to keep stirring over a high heat!

> 2 medium carrots, scraped and thinly sliced lengthways
> $\frac{1}{2}$ × 200 g/7 oz tin baby sweetcorn, drained and halved lengthways
> 1 leek, the white part, washed and thinly sliced lengthways
> $\frac{1}{2}$ small onion, finely chopped
> 25 g/1 oz firm tofu, diced small
> a few button mushrooms, wiped and sliced
> 1 small clove garlic, crushed
> 2 fl. oz home-made vegetable stock (see p. 22), or $\frac{1}{3}$ unsalted vegetable stock cube dissolved
> 2 tbsps orange juice
> $\frac{1}{2}$ tsp unrefined soft brown cane sugar
> 1 tsp soya sauce
> 1 tbsp pure vegetable oil

Before you start, prepare your ingredients.

Heat the oil in a large saucepan or wok until very hot but not smoking. Fry the onion and garlic until transparent but not brown, stirring constantly. Add the carrots and leeks and stir-fry for about 4 minutes. Add the sweetcorn and the mushrooms. Stir-fry for another 3 minutes. Add the beancurd and, stirring, fry for a few minutes. Finally, stir in the stock, orange juice, soy sauce and brown sugar and bring to the boil.

Reduce the heat, stop stirring, cover and simmer for another 4 minutes. Serve on top of brown or white rice. (If you do not use tofu, make sure you use brown rice).

Stir-fry with Peanut
Sauce

I am including a second stir-fry recipe to show how adaptable these recipes are and to encourage you to make your own combinations. It is a delicious and nutritious way to prepare vegetables, since their goodness is completely retained in the quick-cooking method. In this recipe, the peanut dressing coats the vegetables in a way which reminds me of Indonesian food.

1 spring onion, the white part, finely chopped
75 g/3 oz firm tofu, cut into small cubes
75 g/3 oz broccoli, broken into small florets and the thick stalks cut off
2 medium carrots, scraped and sliced thinly lengthways
75 g/3 oz beansprouts
1 tbsp pure vegetable or nut oil, preferably groundnut or sesame
1 dsp smooth peanut butter
dash soy sauce
3 fl. oz boiling water

Have all the ingredients ready prepared before you start cooking.

Dissolve the peanut butter in the boiling water, adding a dash of soy sauce. Keep aside.

Heat the oil in a frying pan or wok until very hot but not smoking. Keeping the heat high, put in the spring onion. Stirring continuously, cook for a minute. Add the carrots and broccoli and stir-fry for 4 minutes. Add the beansprouts and the tofu, and fry for a further 3 minutes. Do not let anything stick to the bottom of the pan.

Pour the peanut butter mixture over the vegetables and

gently stir in. Reduce the heat, cover and simmer for 3 minutes. Serve hot on a bed of brown or white rice. (If you do not use tofu, make sure you use brown rice).

Nut Roast

I don't think that I can get away with a meat-free cookery book without including a nut roast! I resisted the idea for a while because it is so difficult to make such a thing in small quantities. However, I have found a great way to use up what is left over so I think this makes it worth it.

Nut roasts provide an excellent way to get your child to eat nuts which are rich in essential, healthy oils. This can be more difficult than it seems, given that they cannot be fed whole to small children (they are a common cause of fatal choking).

This roast can be served up as it comes or, even better I feel, moistened with a little easily prepared home-made tomato sauce (see p. 33).

> 150 g/5 oz firm tofu, mashed
> 50 g/2 oz mushrooms, wiped and chopped
> 50 g/2 oz fresh wholemeal breadcrumbs
> 50 g/2 oz mixed nuts, ground
> 25 g/1 oz brown rice, cooked
> 1 stick celery, chopped
> $\frac{1}{2}$ small onion, finely chopped
> 1 small free-range egg, beaten
> 1 dsp pure vegetable oil

Preheat the oven to GM5/375°F/190°C.

Rinse the rice in several changes of cold water. Put in a saucepan with about twice its volume of fresh water and bring to the boil. Stir, reduce the heat to a simmer, cover and cook until all the water has been absorbed and the rice is fluffy. If it becomes too dry during cooking, add a little more boiling water.

Meanwhile, heat the oil in a small saucepan and gently fry the onion and celery until soft but not browned. Add the chopped mushrooms and fry for a further 4 minutes or so.

Mix together in a bowl the fried vegetables, cooked rice, ground nuts and breadcrumbs, beaten egg and mashed tofu. Put the mixture in a small greased baking tin or ovenproof dish and bake for 40 minutes. Serve hot with or without tomato sauce. This goes well with a light salad or green vegetable.

Since this is a rich dish, you are likely to have some left over. While some like to eat this cold, sliced up or in sandwiches, I find this somewhat unappetizing. My suggestion is much nicer: try making these delightful little Odd Balls.

> leftover cooked Nut Roast
> 1 free-range egg, beaten
> fresh wholemeal breadcrumbs
> few tsps sesame seeds

Mould the leftover nut roast mixture into small balls. Mix some breadcrumbs with the sesame seeds and put them on a plate. Have the beaten egg ready in a shallow bowl.

Heat the oil in a frying pan until fairly hot. Dip the balls first into the egg and then into the breadcrumb/sesame mixture, coating each one evenly. Put them carefully into the oil and fry on all sides until golden brown. Drain on kitchen roll. Serve hot with a fresh vegetable.

Winter Delight

A nice simple recipe which can be adapted for all sorts of vegetables. The British have never been good with vegetables but I highly recommend cultivating your child's taste for them as soon as possible. Cooked in imaginative ways, they can become a real treat instead of remaining a source of mealtime conflict.

Wherever possible, buy fresh vegetables. Pick the ones which have a good colour and are firm to the touch. Vegetables contain dietary fibre, vitamin C, and essential minerals.

> 1 small parsnip, peeled and diced
> $\frac{1}{4}$ small swede, peeled and diced
> 1 carrot, scraped and diced
> 1 medium potato, scrubbed and diced
> 1 small leek, the white part, washed and sliced
> $\frac{1}{2}$ small turnip, peeled and sliced
> $\frac{3}{4}$–1 pt home-made vegetable stock (see p. 22), or 1 unsalted vegetable stock cube dissolved in boiling water
> 25 g/1 oz butter or margarine
> 25 g/1 oz wholemeal flour
> a little milk if required

Bring the stock to the boil and add all the prepared vegetables except the leek. Bring back to the boil, then turn down and cook on a medium heat for about 5 minutes. Add the leek. Continue to cook for a further 5 minutes or so, or until the vegetables are tender but not breaking up (test with a fork). Drain the vegetables, keeping the stock. If you have less than about half a pint, make this up with milk.

Gently melt the butter or margarine in a saucepan and blend in the flour. Cook for a few minutes, stirring to prevent sticking. Gradually add the stock to the flour, stirring continuously, and then bring to the boil. Let it bubble for a few minutes, then turn down the heat and add the cooked vegetables. Warm them through and then serve on brown rice, bulghur wheat, or wholewheat pasta.

Mixed Vegetable Fricassée

Another easy, adaptable recipe – choose any of your child's favourite vegetables and introduce a few he has yet to try.

1 large carrot, scraped and diced
1 medium courgette, washed and sliced
1 small leek, the white part, washed and sliced
a few small cauliflower florets
$\frac{1}{2}$ small onion, finely chopped
25 g/1 oz butter or margarine or a little pure vegetable oil
25 g/1 oz wholemeal flour

Boil all the vegetables, except the onion, in a little water for 3 minutes. Meanwhile, in a large frying pan, gently melt the butter or margarine. Add the onion and cook until transparent and tender, but not brown.

Drain the vegetables, keeping aside the cooking water. Add the vegetables to the onion and fry gently for a few minutes, stirring frequently to prevent sticking or burning. Blend in the flour, stirring it well with the vegetables. Cook for a further few minutes, then slowly add the cooking water, stirring continuously. Bring to the boil. Reduce the heat and leave the vegetables to simmer until tender but not mushy or overcooked. If you think they are becoming too dry, add a little boiling water.

Serve hot on brown rice or wholewheat macaroni.

Vegetable Crumble

A crumble topping goes well with either Winter Delight (see p. 55) or Vegetable Fricassée (see p. 57). It would taste just as good, however, with vegetables in a plain cheese sauce. This topping is an excellent way of enriching the protein content of the meal by adding nuts cooked in a light, digestible way. Do make sure that the sauce the vegetables are in is nice and thick so that the topping does not collapse into it.

$1\frac{1}{2}$ tbsps sunflower oil
10 g/$\frac{1}{2}$ oz wholemeal flour
10 g/$\frac{1}{2}$ oz wholemeal breadcrumbs
25 g/1 oz oat flakes
25 g/1 oz mixed nuts, ground (you can either buy these in packets, ready ground, or grind your own in a clean coffee grinder or food processor)

Preheat the oven to GM6/400°F/200°C. Prepare the vegetables in their sauce according to the recipe of your choice (eg Winter Delight or Vegetable Fricassée). Pour them into a small ovenproof dish.

In a bowl, mix together the flour, oats and nuts. Add the oil and, with a fork, work it into the dry ingredients until it is light and crumbly. Sprinkle this mixture over the vegetables. Bake in the oven until the topping is golden brown (approx. 15–20 minutes). Serve hot.

Toad-in-the-Hole

The vegetarian sausages now available in the shops are suprisingly tasty and are one of the few convenience foods of which I approve. Toad-in-the hole has always been popular with children, so I see no reason why non-meat-eaters cannot enjoy it too! This recipe can be prepared very quickly using the grill rather than the oven, and the use of some wholemeal flour makes the batter nutritious rather than simply filling.

4 vegetarian sausages, or 'vegebangers'
1 free-range egg
25 g/1 oz plain flour
25 g/1 oz wholemeal flour
1 tsp baking powder
$\frac{1}{2}$ small onion, finely chopped
5 tbsps milk
pure vegetable oil for frying

Heat the oil in a small deep frying pan and gently fry the onion and sausages until the latter are lightly browned on all sides.

Meanwhile, sieve the flours into a mixing bowl. Make a well in the centre and add the egg. With a wooden spoon, mix in the egg, gradually bringing in the flour around the edge. Then slowly add the milk, finally beating it to a smooth batter. Turn on the grill and let it get hot.

When the sausages are cooked, cut them into bite-size pieces (or leave them whole for the older child) within the pan, then turn the heat up high and pour the batter over them. Do not stir but leave for 2–3 minutes until the bottom is brown (but not burnt) and the batter is beginning to set and bubble slightly. Immediately put the pan under the grill leaving enough room for the batter to rise a little and not too close to burn it. (Watch out for flammable handles on frying pans and re-member how hot metal ones get!) Leave it to puff up and turn golden brown (5–10 minutes depending on your grill). Cut and serve hot in sections, with a fresh vegetable.

Huevos Rancheros

This is my version of the scrumptious traditional Mexican American breakfast – 'ranch-style eggs'. It may seem like breakfast to the Americans, but really constitutes a full meal for an English child (or adult for that matter). This recipe would normally call for fried or poached eggs but in the light of fears about salmonella poisoning, it might be wise to use an omelette or firmly scrambled eggs.

For this recipe, you need to have already made a pinto bean hash, but don't be put off: you can make lots of this well in advance and freeze what you are not using immediately. You can also use up leftovers in all sorts of ways (see below for some ideas). The quantity of hash given here will make about 4 adult portions (6–8 children's portions depending on their appetites). While you might not find pinto beans at the supermarket, health food shops stock them and it is worth searching for them – it is not for nothing that they are sometimes known as the 'king of the beans'.

To make the hash:

225 g/8 oz pinto beans, rinsed and soaked overnight

Rinse the beans in several changes of cold water, and remove any stones or odd-looking beans. Cover with cold water and soak overnight.

Boil up the beans in about three times their volume of water (add to the soaking water, rather than throwing it away), then turn down and bubble gently for as long as it takes for them to be totally tender and beginning to fall apart. (This may take anything from 45 minutes–2 hours depending on the beans.) Do not add salt. Check the pan from time to time and add more boiling water if necessary. When they are very soft, drain the beans, reserving the liquid.

Put the beans through a blender or food processor, adding a little of the reserved liquid, to give a soft moist purée. Add a tiny pinch of salt. This mixture can be frozen, or reheated the following day.

To make 2 portions of 'Huevos Rancheros':

2 heaped tbsps pinto bean hash
2 wholemeal Arabic breads/or chapati/or pitta

bread/or muffins ($\frac{1}{2}$ of any of these might be enough for a small child)

2 free-range eggs, scrambled or made into an omelette

25 g/1 oz wholemeal flour

25 g/1 oz margarine or butter

25 g/1 oz Cheddar, or other hard cheese, grated

$\frac{1}{4}$–$\frac{1}{2}$ pt milk

Gently warm up the bean hash in a small saucepan. Warm up the wholemeal breads in the oven.

Meanwhile, make a cheese sauce by gently melting the butter in a small saucepan and blending in the flour. Cook for a minute or two, stirring. Gradually add about $\frac{1}{4}$ pint milk and bring to the boil, stirring continuously. Reduce the heat and stir in the cheese. Cook for a further few minutes. If the sauce seems too thick, add a little more milk. Cook the eggs.

Assemble the meal by spreading 1 tablespoon of hash onto each bread, putting the omelette or scrambled egg on top of it and then pouring cheese sauce over the whole lot.

Leftover hash, in South America, is used to make the ubiquitous 'refritos' or 'Refried Beans' (see below). Alternatively, use as a filling for another Mexican dish, 'Tacos' (see p. 62). Even more simply, warm through and use as a dip with corn chips or wholemeal pitta breads (parents might like to spice up theirs with chili sauce and seasoning).

Refried Beans

leftover pinto bean hash

1 clove garlic, crushed

$\frac{1}{2}$ small onion, finely chopped

1–2 skinned, chopped tomatoes (skin by immersing in boiling water)

pinch oregano
a little pure vegetable oil

Heat the oil in a frying pan and gently fry the garlic and onion until transparent and tender. Add the bean hash, the tomatoes and oregano. Cook gently for 15 minutes, stirring occasionally. Serve hot with an egg; or as a dip with some Mexican corn chips.

Mexican Tacos

This dish is a way of using up leftovers either from a kidney or pinto bean dish, or a TSP (textured soya protein) recipe. However, if there are more than two or three of you to cook for, it is definitely worth making the dish from scratch.

Tacos are fried and shaped corn tortillas (rather like crisp pancakes) which can be filled with various things; they are great fun for children over about $2\frac{1}{2}$ years. A certain amount of manual dexterity is required to get the filled tortilla to the mouth without dropping everything out! Yes, a bit messy but delicious. Children love piling things on their own plate and this dish provides them with bits and pieces to sprinkle on top themselves.

In Mexico, the filling is usually minced beef, but there is no reason not to use a satisfying vegetarian alternative. A child will probably only manage one filled taco shell, so keep unused tacos wrapped in cellophane in the cupboard.

1 packet (12) taco shells
Filling: each taco will need a couple of dessertspoons of one of the following:–
pinto bean hash (see 'Huevos rancheros'
recipe, p. 59)

> *or* cooked kidney beans (see 'Kidney bean
> casserole', p. 39. Use the leftovers as
> they come or mash them up)
> *or* TSP sauce (see the sauce in 'Pasta Pasta',
> p. 67; or the filling for the 'Sussex Roll',
> p. 66)
> *Topping*: use all or some of the following:—
> lettuce, shredded; tomatoes, chopped;
> Cheddar or other hard cheese; grated
> avocado, mashed with sour cream or
> natural yoghurt, or simply sliced
> 1 tsp of tomato ketchup

Heat up your leftovers for the filling (or make a filling following one of the recipes given above). If it is too thin, bring to the boil, reduce heat and simmer uncovered, stirring occasionally, until the liquid is reduced and the mixture has thickened. Meanwhile, prepare the ingredients for the toppings.

Heat the taco shells in the oven as per packet instructions. Fill the hot tacos with 1–2 dessertspoons of the filling. Serve the toppings separately (I like to have them all!) and let the children pile them on top, crowning the whole thing with a teaspoon of tomato ketchup.

TSP (Textured Soya Protein)

TSP is a processed soya-bean product which can be used in vegetarian cooking as a direct substitute for meat — in fact, it contains more protein than meat. It comes in dehydrated forms, in 'natural' or 'savoury' flavours, and can be used in much the same way as mince or meat chunks. I prefer to use the savoury mince.

Although experienced vegetarian cooks may not feel much need for TSP, it is a useful food for parents who are gradually cutting down on meat or are recent converts to meat-free cooking. If you have any worries about protein intake, here are some recipes using TSP.

Moussaka

This is not strictly moussaka since I have omitted the aubergines. Unless they are puréed in some form, they seem a little sophisticated for most small children.

When using TSP, remember that it swells enormously during cooking, so do not be tempted to use too much. Since you are using an oven for this recipe, I have allowed for 4 servings.

225–350 g/8–12 oz potatoes, peeled and sliced thinly
25–50 g/1–2 oz mushrooms, wiped and chopped
35 g/1$\frac{1}{2}$ oz Cheddar (or other hard cheese), grated
25 g/1 oz TSP savoury mince
1 free-range egg, beaten
2 tomatoes, skinned (immerse briefly in boiling water first) and chopped
$\frac{1}{2}$ small onion, finely chopped
1 small clove garlic, crushed
5 heaped dsps Greek strained natural yoghurt
pinch of freshly chopped or dried parsley, or oregano
1 tsp tomato purée
1 dsp olive oil
$\frac{1}{4}$ pt boiling water

Preheat the oven to GM4/350°F/180°C.
Heat the oil in a saucepan until quite hot. Fry the onions until

transparent, stirring to prevent sticking or browning. Add the crushed garlic, chopped tomatoes, tomato purée, boiling water, mushrooms, TSP and herbs. Bring to the boil, stirring. Reduce the heat, cover and simmer for 10−15 minutes.

Meanwhile, peel and boil the potatoes for 8−10 minutes. Drain. When cool enough to handle, slice thinly. Lay the potatoes in the bottom of a small, deep casserole dish. When the TSP mixture is ready, pour over the potatoes.

Beat together the yoghurt, beaten egg and grated cheese and pour over the top. Bake in the oven for 30−40 minutes until set and browned on top.

Serve hot with a fresh vegetable.

Cottage Pie

Just because you do not eat meat, there is no reason you shouldn't enjoy this traditional English dish, especially since it was always a children's favourite.

275 g/10 oz potatoes, cooked and mashed
25 g/1 oz TSP savoury mince
$\frac{1}{2}$ small onion, finely chopped
$\frac{1}{2}$ × 400 g/14 oz tin Italian peeled plum tomatoes, drained and chopped
1 large carrot, scraped and chopped
1 tsp tomato purée
$\frac{1}{2}$ tsp yeast extract
$\frac{1}{4}$ pt home-made vegetable stock (see p. 22), or $\frac{1}{3}$ unsalted vegetable stock cube dissolved in boiling water
1 dsp pure vegetable oil
25 g/1 oz butter
pinch of dried herbs (eg parsley, dill, thyme)

Cook and mash the potatoes with a knob of butter. Heat the oil in a saucepan until fairly hot and fry the onion and carrots until tender, stirring occasionally to prevent burning. Add the TSP, stock, tomatoes, tomato purée, yeast extract, and herbs. Bring to the boil, stirring. Reduce the heat, cover and simmer for about 15 minutes. If it seems too runny, simmer a little longer; if too dry, add a touch more boiling water.

Transfer the mince to a heatproof dish and top with the mashed potato. Dot with a little butter and brown under a hot grill. Serve hot with a fresh vegetable.

Sussex Roll

This is my version of an elongated Cornish pastie. It is much easier to make than little pasties and, with packet pastry, not the least bit daunting. Leftovers can be eaten cold the next day.

Yeast extract is a useful addition to all sorts of stews and casseroles, being rich in minerals and vitamins, especially B vitamins.

25 g/1 oz TSP savoury mince
1 large carrot, scraped and chopped
1 large potato, peeled and diced
$\frac{1}{2}$ small swede, peeled and diced
$\frac{1}{2}$ small onion, finely chopped
$\frac{1}{2}$ tsp yeast extract
1 free-range egg, beaten, or milk, for coating
$\frac{1}{2}$ × 225 g/8 oz packet frozen wholemeal shortcrust
pastry
1 dsp pure vegetable oil
$\frac{1}{4}$ pt vegetable stock made from the vegetable cooking water and $\frac{1}{3}$ unsalted vegetable stock cube

Preheat the oven to GM5/350°F/180°C.
Cook the swede, carrot and potato in boiling water until just

tender but still firm (they should not be falling apart). Drain, keeping aside $\frac{1}{4}$ pint of the vegetable water.

Heat the oil in a saucepan until fairly hot, then gently fry the onion until transparent and tender, stirring occasionally to prevent sticking. Dissolve the piece of stock cube in the vegetable water and add to the onions with the TSP and yeast extract. Bring to the boil, stirring occasionally.

If the mixture seems too wet, simmer a little longer. Take off the heat and gently fold in the cooked vegetables. Leave the mixture to cool for 5–10 minutes.

Meanwhile, roll out the pastry on a floured surface until you have a large thin rectangle. Lay the cooled filling along the middle, slightly off-centre. Paint the edge nearest the mixture with either beaten egg or milk, then fold the pastry over, sealing it along this edge and the two sides to make a big envelope.

Grease a flat baking tray with oil and, with two fish slices, carefully lift the pastry roll on to it. Brush the whole surface with the rest of the beaten egg or with milk. Bake in the oven for about 30 minutes until golden. Serve immediately.

Pasta Pasta

TSP also goes very well with pasta in almost any combination. One can use it to make a traditional bolognese-type sauce for spaghetti, macaroni or pasta shapes, but I think it tastes even better when blended with a cheese sauce.

> 75–100 g/3–4 oz wholewheat pasta (a current favourite of mine is fresh wholewheat ravioli filled with ricotta cheese)
> 25 g/1 oz TSP savoury mince
> 50 g/2 oz Cheddar or other hard cheese, grated
> $\frac{1}{2}$ × 400 g/14 oz tin Italian peeled plum tomatoes, mashed or liquidized with their own juice

25 g / 1 oz butter or margarine
25 g / 1 oz wholemeal flour
$\frac{1}{2}$ pt milk
$\frac{1}{2}$ small onion, finely chopped
1 small clove garlic, crushed
1 tsp tomato purée
1 dsp olive or pure vegetable oil
pinch of fresh or dried herbs (oregano, parsley,
    basil)
$\frac{1}{3}$ pt home-made vegetable stock (see p. 22), or $\frac{1}{3}$
    unsalted vegetable stock cube dissolved in boil-
    ing water

Heat the oil in a saucepan and fry the onion and garlic until transparent and softened, stirring occasionally to prevent sticking. Add the TSP, tomatoes, tomato purée, stock and herbs and bring to the boil. Turn down the heat, cover and simmer for about 15 minutes.

Meanwhile, make a sauce. Gently melt the butter in a small saucepan and blend in the flour. Cook, stirring, for a few minutes. Slowly add the milk, and bring to the boil. Reduce the heat, add the grated cheese, and cook for a further few minutes. Put aside.

Cook the pasta in boiling water until tender but not falling apart. Drain. Put the mince in the bottom of a heatproof dish. Spoon the pasta over it and, finally, pour cheese sauce over the top. If you want to brown the top, sprinkle a little grated cheese over it and put under a hot grill for a few minutes. Serve hot.

MAIN MEALS:
FISH

Properly cooked, fish is exciting and varied; it is a wonderful source of protein, vitamins, minerals and those essential oils which support and build our nervous systems. It is not simply an old wives' tale that fish is 'brain food'.

The secret of cooking most fish is simple: never boil, nor overcook it. Simmering, in the case of fish, means getting the liquid in which it is cooking to a temperature at which its surface barely moves. It does not mean bubbling away at a soft boil. Fish is cooked when the flesh just comes away from the bones; if filleted, it should separate easily when felt with a knife, without falling apart.

When choosing fresh fish, select those which are firm to the touch, have bright eyes, shining scales, a good colour and bright red gills. Avoid lack-lustre fish with floppy bodies and dull, bleary eyes. Ask your fishmonger to clean, skin and fillet fish for you; get him to order those things which you require and he does not appear to stock. Children can develop quite sophisticated tastes when allowed to, so don't stop at plaice and cod – be adventurous. My child's current favourites include octopus, smoked salmon and prawns. Needless to say, he is not served salmon on a regular basis, and is quite happy with my fish cakes too!

With regard to safety in storing and keeping fish at home, it is wise to observe the following rules:

– unwrap fish (do not leave in plastic bags) and keep it in a deep dish away from cooked foods
– eat fresh fish on the day of purchase; do not freeze it
– if fish is bought frozen, put it in the deep freeze within $1\frac{1}{2}$ hours of purchase; if longer than this, eat immediately rather than re-freezing

Make sure that you check fish carefully for stray bones before serving it to a child. If, by some misfortune, a bone does get stuck in a child's throat, you will find that plenty of liquid and dry bread will usually shift it, so don't panic.

Most of my fish dishes use parsley, for several reasons: first, and most importantly, it tastes marvellous with fish; second, its use lays the ground for introducing other herbs later (children can be very tiresome about picking little bits out of their food if they are not used to seasonings); and, last, parsley is perfectly bursting with goodness – it is particularly high in vitamins, E, B and C, and such minerals as iron, copper and magnesium.

Fish Florentine

Spinach is a traditional accompaniment for white fish and this recipe is well suited to any white fish, like plaice, cod, whiting or hake. You can use fresh or frozen fish.

2 fillets of plaice or any other white fish
175 g/6 oz spinach, fresh or frozen (choose leaf or balls, rather than block spinach)
75 g/3 oz Cheddar cheese, grated
$\frac{1}{2}$ pt milk
25 g/1 oz butter
1 tbsp wholemeal flour

Rinse the fish in cold water, then simmer it gently in the milk for about 5–7 minutes. Drain, reserving the milk, and leave aside.

Cook the spinach. If frozen, defrost gently over the heat with a knob of butter; if fresh, remove the tough central stalks, tear the leaves roughly, wash and cook gently without added water until thoroughly wilted. (Be careful not to let it burn.) Chop it up and put the spinach on the bottom of a heatproof dish.

Make a sauce by gently melting the butter in a small saucepan and blending in the flour. Cook for a few minutes, then gradually add the reserved milk (which you will have made up to $\frac{1}{2}$ pint with more milk if necessary), stirring continuously. Bring to the boil. Reduce the heat, add most of the cheese, and simmer for a few more mins.

Flake the fish, checking for bones, on to the spinach. Pour the sauce over the fish. Sprinkle the remaining cheese on top and brown under a hot grill. Serve with potatoes.

Fishy Morsels

Large lumps of fried fish can be daunting for a small child. For this recipe I have chosen the rather unusual 'skate nobs' or 'cod cheeks'. Both of these are bite-sized lumps of delicious firm white fish which contain no small bones at all; they are quite delicious and marvellous value. You will usually have to order them from your fishmonger, but it is worth it. If you really cannot get them, then any firm white fish cut into strips will do too.

> 350 g / 12 oz skate nobs, cod cheeks or monkfish (or
> 2 fillets of other white fish like plaice, cod, hake)
> 1 tbsp wholemeal flour
> 1 free-range egg, beaten
> fresh wholemeal breadcrumbs
> pure vegetable oil for shallow frying

Rinse the fish in cold water and dry on kitchen roll. With a sharp knife, cut away any bones on the skate nobs; if you are cooking fillets, cut them into $\frac{1}{2}$" strips. Check for bones as you go. Roll the pieces first into flour, then into beaten egg. Finally, coat with breadcrumbs.

Heat the oil in a wide saucepan until fairly hot. Drop the pieces of coated fish into the oil and fry for about 5 minutes, turning once, until crisp and golden. Drain off excess oil on kitchen roll. Serve hot with a fresh vegetable and potatoes.

Octopus Rice

I expect many of you will be surprised to find octopus in a children's cookbook, but I beg you not to pass on too hastily. You can buy it in tins (ask your delicatessen to get it for you if it is not on the shelves) or fresh from the fishmonger. The latter, however, requires some dedication to clean, so I should stick to the tinned stuff. It is a remarkable hit, not only with my son, but his guests too, having a firm texture similar to squid.

1 × 110 g tin octopus in soya oil (Isabel, a Spanish brand, is the only one I know), drained and chopped

100 g/4 oz brown or white Basmati rice

1 small onion, finely chopped

50 g/2 oz *petits pois*, or garden peas

Rinse the rice thoroughly in several changes of cold water. Bring it to the boil in twice its volume of water. Stir, cover and simmer the rice until it is fluffy and the water is totally absorbed. (This will take considerably longer for brown rice.) Add a little more boiling water if the water has absorbed before the rice is fully cooked. Drain off any excess water and leave to cool.

Meanwhile, cook the peas. Drain off the oil from the octopus, keeping a little aside. Heat this oil in a large frying pan, then fry the onion until tender and golden. Add the cooked rice, the peas and the octopus (which is already cooked), stir gently with a fork and heat through. Serve hot.

Tuna Bake

Fatty fish like tuna are especially good for growing children, being rich in essential oils. If you use canned fish, do try and buy the brands in brine or a specified oil such as olive or soya, rather than unspecified 'edible oils'.

> 225 g/8 oz potatoes, cooked and mashed
> 1 × 200 g/7 oz tin tuna fish in brine (or red salmon)
> 50 g/2 oz Cheddar or other hard cheese, grated
> $\frac{1}{2}$ small tin of condensed mushroom, celery, or leek soup (make sure you choose a good brand from a health food shop without artificial additives; preferably without salt too)
> a pinch of freshly chopped or dried parsley
> fresh wholemeal breadcrumbs

Scrub and cook the potatoes, leaving their nutritious skins on if possible. Mash them without milk or butter and stir in the parsley. Lay in the bottom of a heatproof dish.

Meanwhile heat the undiluted soup and flake the tuna fish into it. When warmed through, pour the mixture over the mashed potato. Sprinkle fresh breadcrumbs and grated cheese over the top and brown under a hot grill. Serve with a fresh vegetable.

Cod and Macaroni Cheese

Any firm white fish fillets can be used in this recipe. Fish blends deliciously with macaroni cheese, making the dish more special and adding valuable protein. If you buy frozen, packaged fish, make sure you are buying 'fillets' and not blocks of reconstituted fish which can contain crushed bones, eyes, fins ... Bear it in mind when you buy fish fingers too − look for the word 'fillet'.

> 175 g/6 oz cod fillets (or plaice, hake, whiting, haddock)
> 75 g/3 oz wholewheat macaroni, or small pasta shapes
> 50 g/2 oz Cheddar cheese, grated
> 25 g/1 oz butter or margarine
> 25 g/1 oz wholemeal flour
> $\frac{1}{2}$ pt milk
> a bay leaf

Cook the macaroni in boiling water until tender. Drain.

Meanwhile, put the fish in a large frying pan with the bay leaf and cover with milk. Simmer gently (the surface of the milk should barely move) until tender and flaking, for between 5−8 minutes. Remove from the pan. Reserve the milk and make up to $\frac{1}{2}$ pint. Once it has cooled slightly, flake the fish, checking carefully for bones.

Meanwhile, make a sauce by gently melting the butter or margarine in a saucepan and blending in the flour. Cook for a few minutes. Slowly, add the milk, stirring continuously. Bring to the boil and cook for a further few minutes. Reduce the heat, add the cheese. (If the sauce is too thick, add a little more milk.) Carefully stir in the flaked fish and cooked macaroni. Heat through and serve.

A delicious variation on this recipe is to use spinach instead of fish. Use frozen leaf or balls of spinach. Defrost it gently over the heat with a knob of butter. When ready, add it to the sauce with the macaroni.

Salmon Fritters

Tuna could also be used for these fritters but I think salmon is lighter, which makes them even tastier.

> 75–100 g/3–4 oz tinned red salmon or tuna in brine, drained
> 50 g/2 oz self-raising flour (or add 1 tsp baking powder to plain flour)
> 1 free-range egg, beaten
> a little milk
> a pinch of freshly chopped or dried parsley
> pure vegetable oil for shallow frying

Make a well in the middle of the flour and pour the egg and a little milk into it. With a wooden spoon, gradually mix the flour into the egg and milk by drawing in the flour from around the edges. Beat well so that the batter is thick but smooth (do not add so much milk that it is runny). Stir in the flaked salmon and the parsley.

Heat enough oil to cover thinly the bottom of a frying pan. When hot, add tablespoonfuls of the mixture and fry gently until golden on both sides. Drain on kitchen roll and serve hot with a fresh vegetable.

Kedgeree

Without the heavy seasoning characteristic of this Anglo-Indian dish, kedgeree makes a lovely meal for children. It is a light and easy way to eat fish. This is one of the few recipes I use which actually tastes better with white Basmati rice; it is also unusual in that it tastes even better on re-heating! If you are using frozen, smoked fish, do make sure that you are selecting a brand without artificial colourants.

100 g/4 oz Basmati white rice
$\frac{1}{2}$ small onion, finely chopped
1 large smoked haddock fillet (try smoked mackerel for a change)
1 free-range egg
25 g/1 oz butter or margarine
a pinch of freshly chopped or dried parsley
some milk/water

Rinse the rice thoroughly in several changes of cold water. Bring the rice to the boil in twice its volume of water. Turn down the heat, stir, cover and simmer until tender, fluffy and all the water is absorbed. (Use less rather than more water if you are unsure, adding more boiling water as necessary, since it is important that the rice for this recipe is not overcooked.) Transfer the rice to a bowl and let it cool down.

Meanwhile, cover the fish with a mixture of milk and water (about 50:50) and simmer very gently for about 5 minutes. Drain and, once it has cooled sufficiently, flake the fish, discarding any skin and stray bones.

Hard boil, shell and chop an egg. Melt the butter and fry the onion gently until soft – do not let it brown. Add the cooked rice, flaked fish, chopped egg and parsley. Turn carefully with a fork and heat through. Serve warm.

Bulghur Fish Cakes

Bulghur used only to be sold in health food shops but is now sneaking into the supermarkets. Made from wheat, it has excellent nutritional value, supplying iron, vitamin B and phosphorus. It makes an interesting alternative to rice and, in this recipe, gives a pleasant texture to the fish cakes.

1 large fillet of haddock (or any other firm white fish
   like plaice, cod, whiting, hake)
5 fl. oz milk
75 g/3 oz bulghur wheat, cooked
25 g/1 oz wholemeal flour
25 g/1 oz butter or margarine
pinch of freshly chopped or dried parsley
pure vegetable oil for frying
wholemeal flour for coating

Rinse the fish in cold water. Put in a small deep pan and cover
with the milk. Simmer very gently (the surface of the milk
barely swirling) until the fish is tender but not falling apart, for
between 5–8 minutes. Remove from the pan, reserving the
milk. When cool enough to handle, flake the fish, checking
carefully for bones and skin.

Meanwhile, rinse the bulghur wheat and bring to the boil
in twice its volume of water. Cover and simmer for about
10 minutes, until all the water is absorbed.

Make a sauce by gently melting the butter and blending in
the flour. Cook for a few minutes. Slowly add the milk the fish
was cooked in and, stirring continuously, bring to the boil. Add
the parsley.

In a bowl, mix together the flaked fish, the sauce and the
cooked bulghur. Leave the mixture to cool. With floured hands,
shape into cakes, then coat in wholemeal flour. Heat enough
oil to cover the bottom of a frying pan and fry the cakes until
golden on both sides. Drain on kitchen roll. Serve warm with a
fresh vegetable.

The mixture keeps well, so if you have too much, keep it
covered in the fridge and cook for breakfast with a fried egg on
top.

Old-fashioned Fish
▬ Cakes ▬

Although the preceding recipe for bulghur fish cakes is more unusual than good old-fashioned ones made with potato, I cannot resist including these, since they are such favourites and always provide a marvellous way of using up excess mashed potatoes.

225 g/8 oz, or a couple of fillets, fresh or frozen white fish (cod, haddock, whiting, plaice, hake), or any leftovers from a previous meal, like monk-fish, turbot, trout, salmon etc. For a change, try mixing in some smoked fish.

450 g/1 lb potatoes, cooked and mashed (with nutritious skins left on if possible)

1 free-range egg, beaten

wholemeal flour to coat

freshly chopped or dried parsley

pure vegetable oil for shallow frying

a little milk/water for cooking the fish

a bay leaf

Scrub, cook and mash the potatoes.

Put the fish in a pan and just cover with milk and water. Add a bay leaf. Simmer very gently (the surface of the liquid barely moving) for about 5–8 minutes until tender but not falling apart. Do not overcook. Remove the fish from the milk, and when cool enough, flake, removing carefully any bones and skin.

In a bowl, combine the flaked fish, mashed potato, beaten egg and parsley. With floured hands, form the mixture into small cakes and coat in the flour.

Heat enough oil to cover the bottom of a frying pan and fry

the cakes until golden brown on both sides. Drain on kitchen roll. Serve with a fresh green vegetable, like spring greens, cabbage, or broccoli.

This mixture keeps well, so put any leftovers in the fridge and serve the following day for breakfast with a poached egg on top.

Haddock in Creamy Tomato Sauce

This recipe uses a mild and creamy sauce, which is quick and easy to prepare.

> 2 haddock fillets (or any other firm white fish, like cod, hake, plaice, whiting)
> $\frac{1}{2}$ pt milk
> 25 g/1 oz butter or margarine
> 25 g/1 oz wholemeal flour
> 1 tsp tomato purée
> a bay leaf
> a pinch of freshly chopped or dried parsley

Rinse the fillets and simmer them gently (the surface of the liquid should barely be moving) in the milk with the bay leaf and parsley, until tender but not falling apart (about 5−8 minutes). Drain, reserving the milk for the sauce. When cool enough to handle, flake the fish, discarding any skin and checking very carefully for any stray bones.

Gently melt the butter in a saucepan and blend in the flour. Cook for a few minutes, then gradually add the milk, stirring continuously to avoid lumpiness. Add the tomato purée and bring to the boil. Turn down the heat and simmer for a further few minutes. Carefully stir in the flaked fish.

Serve warm with brown rice or mashed potatoes, and a fresh vegetable.

Fish and Millet
Croquettes

Millet is richer in vitamins, and has a higher mineral, protein and fat content, than any other grain. However, most of us have probably never cooked with it, possibly because its bland taste makes it difficult to deal with satisfactorily. These croquettes use millet perfectly. Incidentally, if you substitute cooked oatmeal for millet, you get something very similar to traditional Yorkshire fish cakes.

175 g/6 oz white fish fillets (frozen whiting fillets are perfect for this recipe)
100 g/4 oz millet
75 g/3 oz Cheddar or other hard cheese, grated
$\frac{1}{2}$ small onion, finely chopped
$\frac{1}{2}$ pt water
a good pinch of freshly chopped parsley
vegetable oil for shallow frying
fresh wholemeal breadcrumbs or wheatgerm, to coat
1 free-range egg, beaten
a little milk

Rinse the millet in several changes of cold water. Boil $\frac{1}{2}$ pint water and stir in the millet. Bring back to the boil, then turn down and simmer, stirring frequently, until all the water is absorbed (approx. 30 mins).

Meanwhile, gently simmer the fish in a little milk and water (the surface of the liquid must not bubble, but barely swirl around). When tender, but not falling apart (after 5–8 minutes), remove from the pan and, when sufficiently cooled, flake, removing any bones and skin.

Heat a little oil in a frying pan and cook the onions until

transparent and tender. In a bowl, mix together the millet, onion, flaked fish and grated cheese. With lightly floured hands, shape the mixture into little croquettes. Dip first into the beaten egg, then the wholemeal breadcrumbs or wheatgerm. Fry in hot oil until golden on all sides. Drain on kitchen paper. Serve hot with a fresh vegetable.

Fish and Potato Bake

A simple, light, nutritious way to serve fish.

225 g/8 oz potatoes, peeled and grated
1 medium fillet white fish (plaice, cod, haddock, whiting, hake), skinned
35 g/1½ oz Cheddar cheese, grated
1 free-range egg
¼ pt milk
a little chopped parsley

Preheat the oven to GM4/350°F/180°C.

Rinse the fish in cold water. With a very sharp knife, remove any skin and, checking carefully for any stray bones, cut into very small pieces. (If you are using frozen fish, give it time to defrost sufficiently.)

Put the potato into the bottom of a medium-sized ovenproof dish with a lid. Scatter the fish pieces on top. Whisk the egg with the milk and parsley. Stir in most of the cheese. Pour this mixture over the potato and fish. Sprinkle the remaining cheese on the top. Put the lid on and bake in the oven for about 45 minutes until the custard has set and the surface is lightly browned. Serve hot with a fresh green vegetable.

Traditional Fish Pie

All sorts of combinations of fresh and smoked fish can be used in a fish pie, and any leftovers tastily used up. Do not worry about making too much, for any pie remaining can be left in the fridge and, the following day, made into fish cakes (see below).

> 450 g/1 lb potatoes, mashed
> 275–350 g/10–12 oz cod or haddock fillets
> 25 g/1 oz butter or margarine
> 25 g/1 oz wholemeal flour
> $\frac{1}{2}$ pt milk, or milk and water
> 1 free-range egg, hard-boiled and chopped
> a bay leaf
> freshly chopped parsley
> a little grated cheese (optional)

Rinse the fish in cold water. Simmer gently in milk, or a mixture of milk and water, for about 5–8 minutes until tender but not falling apart. (Make sure the liquid is simmering, not bubbling.) Remove from the pan and, when cool, flake carefully, removing any skin and bones.

Meanwhile, boil the potatoes, with their skins on if possible. Mash them without butter and milk, and keep aside.

Gently melt the butter in a saucepan and blend in the flour. Cook for a few minutes. Gradually add to the flour the liquid in which the fish was cooked, made up to $\frac{1}{2}$ pint with milk. Stir continuously to avoid lumps forming and bring to the boil. Reduce the heat and simmer for a few more minutes, then remove from the cooker.

Add the chopped parsley, the chopped hardboiled egg and the flaked fish to the sauce. Stir in gently and tip the mixture into an overproof dish. Cover with mashed potato, dot with margarine or butter, or a little grated cheese, and brown under a hot grill. Serve hot with a fresh vegetable.

If there is any pie, left over, keep it in the fridge and, the following day, make it into fish cakes. Mix it all together and, if the mixture seems too runny, thicken it up with more mashed potato or some cooked green peas. Add some grated cheese if you like. Then, simply shape the mixture into small round cakes, dust with flour and fry in shallow vegetable oil until golden on both sides.

Avocado and Prawns
Au Gratin

This is an unusual way to serve avocado, since we are used to eating it cold. Avocado marries beautifully with prawns and together they provide a protein-packed dish. Make sure that an avocado is ripe by pressing it gently at the very top with your thumb. If it doesn't yield, it is much too hard for eating. Fresh, unshelled prawns are always better than frozen ones, if you can find them.

> 175 g/6 oz prawns (preferably fresh), shelled and halved
> $\frac{1}{2}$ avocado, sliced
> 50 g/2 oz Cheddar cheese, grated
> 25 g/1 oz butter or margarine
> 25 g/1 oz wholemeal flour
> $\frac{1}{4}$ pt prawn stock (see below).
> $\frac{1}{4}$ pt milk ($\frac{1}{2}$ pt if using frozen prawns which cannot yield a prawn stock)

Wash and peel the prawns, taking off the heads, tails and shells and pulling out any black threads running down their backs.

To make the prawn stock, simply put these shells and heads in a saucepan, cover with water and boil for 15 minutes. Drain, reserving $\frac{1}{4}$ pt liquid.

Make a sauce by gently melting the butter or margarine in a saucepan and blending in the flour. Stir and let it cook for a few mins. Gradually add the milk and the prawn stock, stirring continuously. Bring to the boil. Reduce the heat a little and add the cheese, cooking for a further few mins until the cheese has melted. (You should have a thick, smooth sauce.)

Lay the prawns on the bottom of a heatproof dish. Arrange the sliced avocado on top. Pour the sauce over the contents in the dish. Sprinkle a little grated cheese on top and brown lightly under a hot grill. Serve on top of brown rice.

Prawn Stir-fry

This is my version of a Chinese stir-fry, using prawns and vegetables. Once you have got the hang of the cooking method, you can experiment with other vegetables, such as beansprouts, baby sweetcorn, mushrooms.

> 175 g/6 oz fresh prawns, shelled
> 1 large courgette, thinly sliced (or about 100 g/4 oz broccoli, broken into small florets)
> 1 carrot, scrubbed and sliced thinly lengthwise
> 1 small clove garlic, crushed
> $\frac{1}{2}$ small onion, finely chopped
> $\frac{1}{3}$–$\frac{1}{2}$ 400 g/14 oz tin Italian peeled plum tomatoes, well mashed up or liquidized
> a pinch of freshly chopped or dried parsley
> 1 tbsp pure vegetable oil

Wash and peel the prawns, removing the heads, tails and shells and pulling out any black threads along their backs.

Prepare the vegetables, slicing the carrots and courgettes thinly (or breaking the broccoli into small pieces).

Using a wok or large frying pan, heat the oil until very hot but not smoking. Put in the garlic, onions and carrots.

Cook, stirring constantly, for about 4 minutes. Add the courgettes or broccoli and stir-fry for a further 3–5 minutes. Add the mashed tomatoes, parsley, and prawns and fry for a further 3 minutes. (If the prawns were originally uncooked, they will require longer cooking, until they turn from grey to white/pink.) Serve with brown or white rice.

Tuna Balls

These moist little tuna balls, adapted from a Spanish bar recipe, are delicious. If your child likes quite dry food, serve them as they come but if you need a sauce, the home-made tomato sauce on p. 33 is perfect.

$\frac{1}{2}$ × 200 g/7 oz tin tuna in brine, drained and flaked
3 heaped tablespoons of fresh wholemeal bread-
   crumbs
1 small free-range egg, beaten
some freshly chopped or dried parsley
5 tbsp vegetable stock or $\frac{1}{4}$ unsalted stock cube
   dissolved in boiling water
wholemeal flour for dusting
1 tbsp olive oil

In a mixing bowl, combine the breadcrumbs, flaked tuna, the beaten egg and parsley. If you think the mixture is too wet, add some breadcrumbs. Shape it into little balls and roll in flour.

Heat the oil in a frying pan and, on a medium heat, brown the tuna balls on all sides. Add the stock, put a lid on the pan, and simmer until all the liquid is absorbed (about 15 minutes). Keep your eye on the pan and move the balls occasionally to prevent burning. Serve with or without tomato sauce, accompanied by potatoes or rice and a vegetable.

MAIN MEALS:
CHICKEN

Chickens contain protein, vitamins and minerals. If you wish to include them in your child's diet, I urge you to buy free-range birds which are rapidly finding their way into the supermarkets.

In the light of the information that about 80% of chilled and frozen chickens are infected with salmonella and between one tenth and one half of chickens contain listeria monocytogenes, here are a few notes on handling and cooking poultry safely.

It is advisable to avoid all cook-chill chicken and always to cook your own: conventional methods of cooking chicken will usually eliminate dangerous bacteria. Do not microwave chicken as this may not destroy listeria or salmonella. To be absolutely sure, I would advise against giving chicken to vulnerable infants and children under about 18 months old.

Be extremely careful about preparing chicken. Store raw chicken at the bottom of the fridge, taking care that the un-cooked juices do not drip on other foods. Thaw frozen birds very slowly in the fridge and use a separate chopping board for preparing it. Wipe kitchen surfaces and utensils and wash your hands between preparing raw chicken and other foods.

Chicken is cooked when, if pierced in the thickest part, juices ooze out looking clear, not pink.

Do not put hot poultry straight from the oven or table into the fridge without cooling it first.

Chicken Stock

If you are using whole chickens, don't waste the carcass, but use it to make a fresh chicken stock. This can be frozen, or kept in the fridge for a day or so, and used as required in many recipes for soups, sauces and casseroles.

> chicken carcass, bones and skin
> 1 onion, chopped
> 1 carrot, chopped
> 1 leek, chopped
> 1 stick celery, chopped
> fresh herbs (parsley, rosemary, thyme)
> a bay leaf

Break up the carcass and put it in a deep saucepan with the chopped vegetables, herbs and a bay leaf. Cover with cold water, bring to the boil, then reduce the heat and simmer for about 45 minutes. Strain. If you are going to use the stock within a few days, keep it in the fridge and, before use, skim off the fat which has floated to the top. If you are going to freeze it, let it cool sufficiently to allow you to take this excess fat off first.

Grilled 'Barbecued' Chicken

This barbecue sauce gives the chicken a deliciously sweet taste which children like.

> 2 free-range chicken breasts, skinned
> 1 dsp soft brown raw cane sugar
> 1 tbsp lemon juice

1 dsp soy sauce
1½ tbsp tomato sauce
pure vegetable oil for brushing chicken

Pre-heat the grill to moderately hot.

With a sharp knife, remove any skin and bone from the chicken pieces. Make the barbecue sauce by mixing together in a bowl the sugar, lemon juice, soy sauce and tomato sauce.

Place the chicken in the grill pan and brush first with a little vegetable oil and then baste liberally with the barbecue sauce. Place under the grill several inches away from the heat. Cook for about 10 minutes, then turn over. Oil and baste the other side in a similar way and grill for a further 10–15 minutes.

Test that the chicken is cooked by piercing it with a sharp knife in the middle – the juices should be clear rather than pink. Do not let the chicken overcook. Serve hot with potatoes or rice and a fresh vegetable.

Chicken Fricassée

2 free-range chicken breasts, skinned
½ small onion, finely chopped
1 leek, white part only, finely chopped
25 g/1oz frozen peas
25 g/1 oz sweetcorn
1 clove garlic, crushed
1 free-range egg yolk (optional)
home-made chicken or vegetable stock (see pp. 89 and 22), or part of an unsalted stock cube dissolved in boiling water
1½ tbsp pure vegetable oil
a pinch of dried herbs (parsley, dill, tarragon or chervil)
a bay leaf

With a very sharp knife, remove any skin and bone from the chicken. Heat the oil until very hot in a deepish frying pan which has a lid. Add the chicken pieces and cook until they are browned and sealed on all sides. Remove from the pan for a minute.

Reduce the heat to medium and put in the chopped onion, leek and crushed garlic. Cook for about 4 minutes, stirring to prevent sticking and burning. Return the chicken pieces to the pan and pour in enough hot stock to cover. (If the stock does not completely cover the chicken, turn the chicken over half way through cooking.) Put the lid on the pan, bring the stock up to the boil, add the bay leaf and herbs, and reduce to a simmer. Cook the chicken in the stock for 30 minutes, then add the peas and sweetcorn. Cook for a further 8 minutes or so.

Test the chicken is cooked by piercing with a knife – there should be no pinkness inside. Remove the chicken pieces and keep warm. Boil the stock for a minute or two, to reduce slightly, then turn heat right down and add the egg yolk, if used. Simmer on a low heat for 5 minutes (do not boil). Serve the chicken on a bed of brown rice and pour the sauce over it.

Country Fried Chicken and Chips

This simple recipe is quite mouth-watering.

> 2 free-range chicken breasts, skinned
> 1 small free-range egg, beaten
> wholemeal flour for coating
> fresh wholemeal breadcrumbs
> pure vegetable oil for deep frying
> pinch of dried herbs (parsley, thyme)

Put the flour on one plate and mix in the herbs. Spread the breadcrumbs out on another. Dip the skinned breasts first into the flour, then into the beaten egg and finally into the breadcrumbs. Try to coat the chicken evenly.

Heat up enough oil in a small deep pan to cover the chicken pieces. Lower the chicken into the hot oil and deep fry for about 10 minutes over a medium heat. The chicken should be golden brown and cooked through (always check with a sharp knife that it is cooked in the middle and no pink juices remain inside). Drain on kitchen roll. Serve hot with fresh vegetables and chips.

There is nothing wrong with having chips occasionally if your child enjoys them, especially if you use good fresh oil and leave the potato skins on. In this case, you may use the oil in which the chicken was fried.

The best way to cook chips is the French way. Heat the oil until very, very hot and immerse the chips. Leave them to cook for a minute or two. Remove from the oil on to kitchen paper. Heat the oil up again until almost smoking and put the chips back for a second time. Remove when golden brown and drain on kitchen paper. I think you will taste the difference between these and traditional English chips!

Stir-fry Chicken

Stir-fry meals are adaptable for vegetables, fish and chicken; they are quick to prepare and full of goodness because rapid cooking prevents the loss of nutrients. The vegetables given below can be varied according to what is available – try, for example, leeks, mushrooms, peas or beansprouts.

1 free-range chicken breast, skinned
2 spring onions, the white parts, finely chopped

50–75 g/2–3 oz broccoli, broken into small florets
1 medium carrot, scraped and finely sliced lengthways
1–2 tbsps pure vegetable oil (sesame oil is especially tasty for stir-frying)
2–3 tbsps vegetable or chicken stock (for such
small amounts I use a corner of an unsalted stock
cube dissolved in boiling water)
1 dsp light soy sauce
cornflour to coat

With a very sharp knife, remove the skin and any bones from
the chicken and cut into very thin strips. Dip in cornflour to
coat. Heat 1 tbsp oil in a large frying pan or wok. When it is
very hot, throw in the chicken pieces and stir-fry for about
4 minutes, turning constantly. Remove from the pan and keep
warm on a plate.

If necessary, heat the remaining oil, then stir-fry the prepared
vegetables for between 3–5 minutes on a high heat, stirring
continuously. Turn the heat down and put the chicken pieces
back. Add about 2 tablespoons of stock and the soy sauce and
stir carefully. Put the lid on and simmer for 2 minutes. Serve on
brown rice or wholewheat noodles.

Chicken and Pineapple

Pineapple is a tasty complement for chicken, and gives it a
naturally sweet taste which appeals to children.

2 free-range chicken breasts, skinned
75 g/3 oz pineapple chunks canned in natural
juice, roughly chopped
75 ml/3 fl. oz pineapple juice, drained from tin
175 ml/7 fl. oz chicken stock (preferably home-

made, see p. 89 or $\frac{1}{3}$ unsalted stock cube dissolved in boiling water)
1 dsp cornflour
a pinch of dried or freshly chopped herbs (parsley,
dill, chervil or tarragon)

Mix together the stock and the pineapple juice and, in a small deep pan, heat up to the point at which it is beginning to bubble. Put in the chicken pieces and herbs, and bring back up to simmering point. Simmer for about 15–20 minutes, until the chicken is tender and cooked (check the middle with a sharp knife and make sure no pink juices come out). Remove the chicken from the pan, cut into slices and keep warm.

Reduce the stock by about $\frac{1}{3}$ by boiling rapidly for several minutes. Thicken by mixing in the cornflour (which has first been blended with a little cold water in a cup). Put the chicken back in the sauce with the pineapple pieces and heat through gently for 3 minutes. Serve on rice or bulghur wheat with a fresh vegetable.

Surinamese Chicken Stew

This is a recipe I have adapted from a traditional South American one. It is eaten on every feast day by the Creoles in Surinam and is one of their few national dishes. When I ate chicken, this was one of my favourites. Use a peanut butter which is completely natural, without any additives such as palm oil (one of the few vegetable oils high in saturated fats). You càn tell the healthy brands of peanut butter because the oil separates from the peanut butter in the jar. This can simply be stirred back in when you want to use it.

2 free-range chicken pieces, boned, skinned and cut into smallish pieces
350 g/12 oz sweet potatoes, peeled
$\frac{1}{2}$ small onion, finely chopped
1 generous dsp smooth peanut butter
$\frac{1}{2}$ pt chicken stock made from the bones and skin of the chicken pieces (see p. 89), or $\frac{1}{2}$ stock cube dissolved in boiling water
1 dsp pure vegetable oil (preferably groundnut)
a pinch of freshly chopped or dried herbs (parsley, dill, chervil or tarragon)

Quarter the sweet potatoes and cook in boiling water for about 5 minutes. Drain and, when sufficiently cooled, slice or dice roughly. Heat the oil in a saucepan and gently fry the onion until tender and transparent. Turn the heat up to medium and add the chicken pieces. Cook for about 5 minutes, stirring frequently, until lightly browned and well sealed on all sides.

Pour the stock over the chicken and bring to the boil. Add the herbs. Reduce the heat and simmer gently for about 15 minutes. Remove a ladleful of the hot stock and, in a cup, blend it with the peanut butter. Stir this into the stock. Put the partly cooked potatoes into the pan, stir carefully and cook for a further 5 minutes or until the potatoes are nice and soft. Serve on brown rice.

Chicken Fritters

After the Sunday roast, many of us want ideas for using up leftover cooked chicken. These simple fritters are made from a healthy buckwheat flour batter which has a light, nutty taste. If you would like a sauce to moisten the fritters, try the home-made tomato sauce on p. 33.

about 75 g/3 oz leftover cooked chicken bits, without skin, diced small
50 g/2 oz buckwheat flour
1 free-range egg
2–3 fl. oz milk
1 tbsp pure vegetable oil
pinch of dried herbs (parsley, dill, chervil or tarragon)

Put the flour and herbs into a mixing bowl. Make a well in the
centre and break the egg into it. Using a wooden spoon, mix
the egg into the flour, gradually drawing in the flour from
around the edges. Gradually add the milk. Beat well to give a
thick smooth batter. Stir in the diced cooked chicken.

Heat the oil in a frying pan until fairly hot, but not smoking.
Drop the mixture in with a dessertspoon and cook on both
sides to a golden brown. Serve hot with vegetables and potato.

Chicken Forestière

Here is a simple sauce with which to jazz up those leftovers
from the roast chicken.

50–100 g/2–4 oz leftover cooked chicken bits,
   diced
50–75 g/2–3 oz button mushrooms, sliced and
   blanched (if your child does not like mushrooms,
   try using frozen sweetcorn and peas)
25 g/1 oz butter or margarine
25 g/1 oz plain white flour
$\frac{1}{4}$ pt chicken stock, preferably home-made, or $\frac{1}{3}$
   stock cube dissolved in boiling water
$\frac{1}{4}$ pt milk

a pinch of dried or freshly chopped herbs (parsley, dill, chervil or tarragon)

Blanch the mushrooms by immersing them for a minute in boiling water (this takes out the blackness which would otherwise discolour your sauce). Drain, slice and put on kitchen roll to absorb the liquid.

Gently melt the butter or margarine in a saucepan and blend in the flour. Cook over a low heat for a minute or so, then gradually stir in the chicken stock, milk and herbs. Bring to the boil and simmer, bubbling, for a few minutes until thickened. Add the mushrooms and cooked diced chicken to the sauce and simmer for 3–4 minutes. Serve on brown rice.

Chicken Risotto

Risottos are lovely all-in-one meals which are moist and full of flavour. However, this flavour depends largely on good stock, so do use home-made stock for this recipe.

50–100 g/2–4 oz (or more) leftover cooked chicken, without skin, thinly sliced or diced small
100 g/4 oz of brown rice or white Italian or Spanish risotto rice, washed
25 g/1 oz frozen peas, cooked
50 g/2 oz frozen sweetcorn, cooked
$\frac{1}{2}$ small onion, finely chopped
1 small clove garlic, crushed
25 g/1 oz butter
$\frac{1}{2}$ pt home-made chicken or vegetable stock (see p. 89 or p. 22)
a bay leaf
a pinch of fresh or dried herbs (parsley, dill, chervil or tarragon)

Melt the butter in a heavy-bottomed pan or medium-sized frying pan with a lid. Fry the onions and garlic gently until transparent and softened. Add the rice and cook for a minute or so, stirring frequently. Pour in the stock and add the bay leaf and any herbs. Bring to the boil, stir once, turn down the heat, and cover. Simmer gently until all the liquid is absorbed and the rice is cooked (about 20 minutes).

Meanwhile, cook the peas and sweetcorn. Drain. When the rice is ready, carefully fold in the cooked sweetcorn, peas and chicken bits. Replace the lid and cook gently for a further 5 minutes. Serve hot.

LIGHT MEALS AND SUPPERS

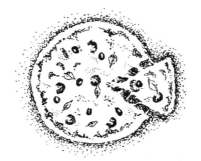

It is always useful to have lots of ideas for light meals – using ingredients you always have in the house like eggs, cheese and potatoes – and for spreads/dips to put on toast or eat with raw vegetables. (I think we could all do with a change from marmite, honey and peanut butter, good though they all are.) A little thought, a minimum of time, and some inspiration can make supper time a pleasure rather than an exasperation.

Spreads and dips are particularly useful in the summer months when nice fresh salad vegetables are available. These can be attractively served as *crudités*, in addition to wholemeal toast or bread. Choose prime, fresh vegetables and cut them up into strips (cucumber, carrot, red pepper, celery) or slice them (mushrooms, tomatoes, avocado, apple).

Avocado Mousse

Avocado pears are extremely nutritious, being rich in vitamins, minerals, protein and unsaturated fat. On their own they can be a little bland but, blended with cream cheese, produce a delicious creamy spread.

> 1 ripe avocado (test by gently pressing the top end with your thumb – if it is hard, it is not ready to eat)
> 100 g/4 oz cream or curd cheese, or natural *fromage frais*, or Greek strained natural yoghurt
> 1 tsp lemon juice

Halve the avocado, remove the stone and scoop out the flesh. In a bowl or hand blender, mash or purée together all the ingredients. Serve on or with wholemeal toast and with washed and sliced raw vegetables for dipping. Keep what is left over in the fridge, covered tightly with clingfilm, close to the surface to prevent discolouration.

Aubergine Pâté

Aubergines contain valuable vitamin B, and have a light taste and creamy texture when baked. Without the skins on, they do not have a pronounced flavour, so are quite suitable for children. Don't be afraid to accustom your child to garlic — abroad they eat it from the cradle!

  1 medium aubergine
  25 g/1 oz butter (or 1 dsp strained Greek yoghurt)
  1 small clove garlic, crushed
  a pinch of dried parsley
  1 tsp lemon juice

Preheat the oven to GM5/375F/190°C. Prick the aubergine with a fork and place on a baking tray. Cook for about 45 minutes until soft and wrinkled. When cool enough to handle, peel, or cut in half and scoop out the flesh. Put it in the blender with the butter (or yoghurt), parsley, garlic and lemon. Serve warm or cold with wholemeal toast or warm wholemeal pitta or Arabic bread.

Hummus

Home-made hummus always tastes better than shop-bought in my opinion; it is also much cheaper! Chick peas are full of iron, calcium and vitamins and, prepared in this way, easily digestible.

> 100 g/4 oz chick peas, washed and soaked overnight
> 2 tbsp tahini (sesame seed paste)
> 1 small clove garlic, crushed
> juice of a small lemon

Cook the soaked chick peas by bringing them to the boil in fresh water, then simmering until soft (an hour or so). Drain the peas, keeping aside a little of the cooking water.

Put the peas in a blender with a little of the cooking water, the tahini, garlic and lemon. Blend until very smooth, adding a little more cooking water if it is too dry.

Chill in the fridge. Serve with wholemeal toast or warm wholemeal pitta or Arabic bread and sliced raw vegetables. Hummus keeps well in the fridge, covered with clingfilm. If it dries out, work in a little olive oil to soften it.

Taramasalata

Home-made taramasalata is far more subtle than many of the bought varieties, which sometimes have pink colourants in them and are bulked up with breadcrumbs.

> 75 g/3 oz smoked cods roe
> 50 g/2 oz cream cheese

1 dsp olive oil
1 tsp lemon juice

Mash or blend all the ingredients together. Chill in the fridge. Serve with wholemeal toast or warm wholemeal pitta or Arabic bread.

Smoky Spread

Oily fish, unlike fatty meat, is good for you. The essential oils in fish are beneficial and are believed to help build up resistance to diseases like heart conditions and multiple sclerosis which can develop later in life. Tinned fish can be a marvellous standby and the basis of many quick recipes. When buying canned fish, try and buy those in specified oils, such as olive or soya, rather than simply 'edible oils'.

1 small tin smoked mussels (or mackerel, smoked oysters, sardines)
75 g/3 oz cream cheese
1 tsp lemon juice

Blend or mash all the ingredients together. Chill in the fridge. Serve on wholemeal toast.

Eggy Bread with Mushrooms

This is a very simple recipe. If you have any cream in the fridge, it makes the whole thing rather special.

> 50 g/2 oz Cheddar cheese, grated
> 1 free-range egg, beaten
> a few mushrooms, wiped
> 1 tbsp single cream (optional)
> pinch of dried herbs (parsley, chervil, chives)
> slices of wholemeal bread
> pure vegetable oil for shallow frying

Brush the mushrooms lightly with oil and put under a hot grill for about 4 minutes until cooked. Slice thinly. Beat the egg with the cream.

Heat a little oil in a shallow frying pan. Dip the bread into the egg mixture and lower gently into the oil. Fry on both sides until golden brown. Remove from the pan and top the bread with mushroom slices and grated cheese. Finish off under a hot grill until the cheese has melted and lightly browned.

North African Potato Cake

The North Africans make omelettes which are more like quiches without the pastry. They can be eaten hot or cold, served on their own or with vegetables, taken on picnics, or even used as a sandwich filling.

> 100–175 g/4–6 oz potatoes, cooked and mashed
> 2 free-range eggs, beaten
> $\frac{1}{2}$ small onion, finely chopped
> a pinch of fresh or dried parsley
> pure vegetable oil for frying

Peel and cook the potatoes until soft. Drain and mash. Fry the onions in a little oil until soft and add them to the potatoes. Mix well. Beat in the eggs and parsley.

Heat a tablespoon of oil in a small frying pan with a flame-proof handle and swish it around the sides to stop the omelette sticking. Pour in the mixture and cook on a low flame for about 10 minutes or so until the bottom sets and browns. Put it under a hot grill to set and brown the top. Turn out on to kitchen roll. Serve in slices either hot or cold.

Vegetable Frittata

Another all-in-one vegetable dish, this time a variation on a Californian dish which, in turn, is a Mexican variation of, I suppose, a Spanish omelette!

This recipe can also be made in advance and refrigerated for 24 hours if desired. Served at room temperature it tastes slightly different but is still great.

> 2 free-range eggs, beaten
> 50 g/2 oz frozen spinach (2 or 3 spinach balls)
> 35 g/1 $\frac{1}{2}$ oz mushrooms, wiped and sliced
> 1 small courgette, finely sliced
> 50 g/2 oz Cheddar cheese, grated
> 1 tbsp olive or other pure vegetable oil

Heat the oil in a non-stick frying pan with an ovenproof handle. Defrost the spinach gently following packet instructions and drain off any excess liquid.

Over a medium heat, fry the courgette until tender (about 4 minutes). Add the mushrooms and cook for 2–3 minutes. Add the spinach.

Whisk the eggs and stir in nearly all the grated cheese. Pour the egg mixture over the vegetables. Reduce the heat slightly and cook for a few minutes until the bottom is set and golden. Sprinkle with the remaining cheese and put under a hot grill until puffed, set and golden on top (3–5 minutes). Turn out on to a plate if possible, or serve in slices from the pan.

Scrambled Egg with Smoked Haddock

You may also use smoked salmon scraps for this recipe – a wonderful breakfast for adults and a good supper for any child! Ask your fishmonger for such scraps – they are usually very cheap. Sort through, discarding hard bits and skin, keeping only the choicest pieces. It is hardly worth making scrambled egg for one, so this is for 2 people.

3 free-range eggs, beaten
75 g/3 oz smoked haddock, cod or salmon
$\frac{1}{4}$ pt milk
knob butter

Heat the fish gently in the milk for 3–5 minutes, then drain, keeping the liquid. Flake the fish, checking carefully for stray bones and skin.

Whisk the eggs with half the cooking milk. Melt the butter in a small non-stick saucepan and add the eggs. Cook over a low heat, stirring continually. Once the mixture begins to scramble, add the flaked fish and continue stirring until the eggs are firm. Serve on wholemeal toast.

Cheese Pancakes

These pancakes are delicious on their own, with a vegetable, or served up with baked beans.

> 1 free-range egg, beaten
> 25 g/1 oz Cheddar (or other hard cheese), grated
> 10 g/$\frac{1}{2}$ oz porridge oats
> 5 g/$\frac{1}{4}$ oz wholemeal flour
> pure vegetable oil for shallow frying

In a bowl, mix together the beaten egg and the grated cheese. Then add the oats and flour. Heat the oil until quite hot then gently drop dollops of mixture into the pan. Turn the heat down and flatten out the pancakes a little with a spatula. Fry for about 3–4 minutes until each side is golden brown. Drain on kitchen roll and serve hot.

Cheese Sausages

This can be a quick supper served with baked beans, or a hearty meal, when served with a home-made tomato sauce (p. 33), potatoes and vegetables. Extremely easy to make, these 'sausages' are mouth-wateringly good!

> 35 g/1$\frac{1}{2}$ oz Cheddar (or other hard cheese), grated
> 75 g/3 oz wholemeal breadcrumbs
> 1 free-range egg
> a pinch of dried herbs (parsley, sage or thyme)
> pure vegetable oil for shallow frying

In a bowl, mix 2 oz of breadcrumbs (keep the rest aside for coating the sausages) with the cheese and herbs. Separate the egg. With a fork, mix the yolk into the cheese mixture. With clean hands, mould the mixture into several sausage shapes.

Beat the white of the egg with a wire whisk until it gives soft peaks. Heat enough oil to cover the bottom of a small frying pan. Dip the sausages first into the egg white and then the breadcrumbs, coating them evenly. Fry on all sides until golden and crisp. Drain on kitchen roll and serve hot.

Instant Pizza

A super, simple supper snack which makes a welcome change from the ubiquitous cheese on toast! You can vary the toppings with different kinds of cheese, tinned fish, and any bits and pieces your child might like.

> *Pizza base (use any one of the following)*:
>   wholemeal muffins (split in half)
>   wholemeal crumpets
>   picnic-size wholemeal pitta breads
> *Topping*: 1 small tomato, skinned and finely
>   chopped
>   mozzarella cheese, thinly sliced
>   some tinned tuna fish, drained and flaked
>   a drizzle of olive oil

Heat the grill and cover the grill pan with foil to catch drips. Toast the pizza bases very lightly on both sides and butter on the topside.

Lay the breads on the grill pan. Put on some flaked tuna, then pile on first the tomato and then the cheese. Drizzle a little olive oil on the top and put under a hot grill (not too near the flame) until heated through and slightly browned. Allow to cool a little before serving as hot cheese can easily burn the mouth.

Creamy Baked Potato

Potatoes are good for you! They are nutritious, rich in dietary fibre and vitamin C. They are high in starch and potassium and low in fat and salt – quite the opposite of potato snacks, in fact. The goodness of a potato is especially concentrated in the skin.

Baked potatoes can also be done beautifully in a *Diable* – a French earthernware vessel which stands on the hob. The potatoes are simply washed, pricked, put inside and left to cook. It produces perfect baked potatoes which taste as they should.

> 1 medium baking potato
> 25–50 g / 1–2 oz cheese, grated
> a knob butter
> drop of milk

Preheat the oven to GM5 / 375°F / 190°C. Prick the potato with a fork and bake in the oven. To speed up cooking, you can push a skewer through the middle (this conducts heat into the centre). A potato is cooked when a fork goes in and out easily.

Halve the potato and carefully scoop out the centre into a bowl without breaking the skin, which is kept aside. Mash the potato with the butter, milk and cheese and then return to the skin. Sprinkle a little grated cheese on the top of each half and put under a hot grill until melted and browned. Serve hot.

You can vary the fillings using this method by mashing the potato with avocado, fromage frais, curd or cream cheese; or try mixing in some flaked tuna fish, sweetcorn or cooked spinach. You may finish off with prawns, grated cheese or slices of mozzarella cheese browned quickly under the grill. For a delightful change, try using sweet rather than ordinary potatoes, baked in their jackets and served simply with butter.

Quick Cheesy Potato

A quick, filling dish – one which traditionally bakes in the oven but adapts well for the hob in this case. You may use old or new potatoes, leaving their skins on wherever possible.

> 450 g/1 lb potatoes, scrubbed, washed and sliced in rounds
>
> 50–75 g/2–3 oz Gruyère (or any other mild similar cheese)
>
> $\frac{1}{4}$ pt milk (including top-of-the-milk or a splash of single cream if possible)

Put the sliced potatoes in boiling water. Reduce the heat slightly and cook until tender but not falling apart. Drain the water off. Turn the heat right down to a simmer. Add the milk/ cream to the pan with the cheese. Heat very gently until the cheese has melted, stirring carefully from time to time. Serve hot with a green vegetable if desired.

Hash Brown and Apple Cake

Fried grated potatoes are standard in America and most uncommon here. The apple adds a special flavour. This cake can be served up with fresh vegetables, or baked beans, or grated cheese and some buttered wholemeal bread.

> 175 g/6 oz potatoes, peeled and grated (do not leave for too long before cooking as they will discolour)
>
> 1 free-range egg, beaten

1 small apple, peeled and grated
$\frac{1}{4}$ small onion, very finely chopped
a pinch of parsley, dill or thyme
pure vegetable oil for shallow frying

In a bowl, mix together the grated potato, apple, onion, herbs and beaten egg. Heat the oil in a frying pan and press the mixture into it, making one large, flat cake. Fry on both sides for about 6 minutes each, until golden brown. Drain on kitchen roll and serve in slices.

Corn-on-the-Cob with Sesame Toast

My son adored corn-on-the-cob from the moment he had sufficient teeth and the manual dexterity to hold the cob properly. This is the simplest of meals, yet so obvious it is frequently overlooked. The beautifully nutty taste of the sesame toast provides a nutritious supplement (sesame contains lecithin which lowers blood chloresterol levels).

corn-on-the-cob
butter or margarine
wholemeal bread
sesame seeds

Pull the outer green husk and the silky beard off the corn cob. Trim the stalk. Put in enough boiling water to easily cover. The corn will cook quicker with a lid on the pan. Boil gently until tender. (Test for tenderness by pushing a sharp fork into the middle of the yellow kernels. If the fork easily pricks and withdraws the corn is cooked.) Remove from the water and run under the cold tap for a minute to cool slightly. Pat dry with kitchen roll, coat lightly with butter or margarine and serve.

Toast one side of a slice of wholemeal bread, then butter the other side right up to the edges. Sprinkle liberally with sesame seeds, pressing them down onto the butter. Toast under a hot grill until golden brown.

'Real' Baked Beans

Like everyone else, I use tinned baked beans occasionally and they are a good source of protein and a marvellous standby. Nevertheless, the home-made kind are always better and just as popular with small children (as long as they are not too used to the canned variety, which are usually sweetened). You can make a larger quantity than this and freeze in meal-size portions.

> 100 g/4 oz haricot beans, rinsed and soaked over-night (or, alternatively, stand in boiling water for an hour, then cook)
> 1 × 400 g/14 oz tin Italian peeled plum tomatoes, thoroughly mashed or liquidized with their juice
> 1 small onion, finely chopped
> 1 small clove garlic, crushed
> 1 tbsp concentrated apple juice
> 1 tbsp pure vegetable oil
> a pinch of mixed dried herbs (parsley, oregano, thyme, basil)

Bring the beans to the boil in the water they have soaked in, adding more if necessary. After about 10 minutes, cover and simmer until soft (about 30–45 minutes). Drain.

Meanwhile, heat the oil and cook the onion and garlic gently until soft. Add the tomatoes, the apple juice and herbs and leave to simmer for 15 minutes. Add the drained beans and simmer for a further 15 minutes. Serve with wholemeal toast, crumpets or muffins.

DESSERTS

My son ate nothing but fruit (sometimes with yoghurt) after his meals until he was over two. Even now, at three, we seldom have desserts – perhaps once at the weekend – and I am quite selective about what I make for him. Nat never tires of fruit – he has as much as he wants and as wide a variety as the seasons allow. Always select the best quality fruit and complain if you are fobbed off with anything less. Fruits need to be washed to remove traces of chemicals but leave the skin on whenever possible since much of their goodness is concentrated just below the surface.

While sugars which occur naturally with fibre, vitamins and minerals in fresh fruit are perfectly healthy, refined sugar provides no nourishment, only 'empty' calories. It makes children fat, rots their teeth and spoils their appetite; it is also addictive. It is therefore important to limit sugar intake. If you are going to give sweet things, better that they should come after a meal: children will want less then and sugar taken this way causes significantly less damage to young teeth.

Fresh Orange Jelly

Children adore jellies and making your own jelly requires no added sugar nor any additives. In the summer, use fresh fruit; in the winter, try interesting fruits, tinned in their own juices rather than syrup.

There are alternatives to gelatine which use no animal products at all (eg agar-agar) which are worth experimenting with. I must admit, though, that the best jelly is still made with gelatine. Use just under a pint of liquid to a 0.4 oz (11 g) sachet of gelatine. This recipe makes about 4–6 children's servings.

> 3 oranges
> $\frac{3}{4}$ pt unsweetened orange juice
> 4 tbsps water
> 11 g/0.4 oz sachet gelatine

Peel the oranges with a sharp knife, removing all the peel, pith and pips. Cut into thin rounds, catching any juice, and arrange in the bottom of a serving dish.

Put 4 tablespoons of boiling water in a cup and sprinkle the gelatine on top (not the other way round). Stir until dissolved. Add this to the orange juice and the juice from the peeled oranges, and make the liquid up to just under a pint with more water if necessary. Stir well. Pour over the orange rounds and put into the fridge to set.

Variations on this recipe are endless, according to which fruits are in season. Use fresh fruit whenever you can and match it with a complementary fruit juice. Here are a few ideas:

> kiwi fruit and peaches in tropical-mix fruit juice
> banana and seedless white grapes in apple juice
> melon and raspberries in white grape juice
> pineapple in pineapple juice

Raspberry Yo-Jelly

An absolutely delicious variation on the traditional jelly, the yo-jelly has the texture of a mousse without using cream. Here, the liquid is a mixture of fruit juice and yoghurt. Adding purées of soft summer fruits makes the jelly even thicker and creamier. Again, the variations are endless and give lots of scope for imagination. Vary the amount of honey added according to the sweetness of the fruits – ripe strawberries may not need any sweetening, but raspberries can be a little sharp when mixed with plain yoghurt.

> 225 g/8 oz raspberries
> $\frac{1}{2}$ pt Greek strained yoghurt
> just over $\frac{1}{4}$ pt white grape juice
> 4 tbsps water
> 11 g/0.4 oz sachet gelatine
> 1 dsp clear runny honey

Add the fruit juice slowly to the yoghurt, stirring well. Mix in the honey. Mash the raspberries with a fork. (Although raspberry pips are quite digestible, I would suggest that black-berries and strawberries should be strained through a sieve for this recipe.)

Put 4 tablespoons of boiling water in a cup and sprinkle the gelatine on top (not the other way round). Stir until dissolved. Add the gelatine and the mashed raspberries to the yoghurt mixture and stir well. Pour in to a serving bowl and set in the fridge.

Exotic Fruit Salad

While some foreign fruits can be a disappointment by the time they reach the shops in this country, others survive the journey well and are a delight to eat. To make an exotic dessert, include some of the following in a fruit salad, along with peaches or nectarines, bananas and seedless grapes.

> Persimmon or Sharon Fruit – A sweet, sticky yellow fruit. Cut off the top and scoop out the pulp with a spoon.
> Fresh Figs – These can be eaten with or without

the skin and have no stone. Make sure they are soft and ripe or they can be dry and boring.

Fresh Dates – These are lovely, and really superior to the sticky Christmas variety. Cut in half and remove the stones, then chop up.

Kiwi Fruit – Peel them carefully, removing as little skin as possible, and slice the bright green flesh in rounds.

Mango – Cut the fruit vertically from the top to the stone, then repeat on the other side. Prise apart and scoop the flesh out from both halves with a spoon.

Ugli Fruit – This looks like a large grapefruit but is a lot sweeter. Peel and segment like other citrus fruits

Lychee – A wonderful sweet white fruit. Remove the brittle skin, and the central stone by cutting in half.

Melon – The numerous varieties of melon now available should be used for more than the occasional starter to a meal. They are succulent and juicy and, in season, quite cheap.

Pineapple – Although fresh pineapple is wonderful, it is not an easy fruit to prepare correctly without losing large amounts of flesh. It is also quite difficult to detect one in perfect condition. If you don't feel confident, I would buy tinned pineapple in its own juice.

Prepare the fruits and put them in a large serving bowl. Sprinkle with a little lemon juice, orange juice and water. If you think the juice tastes sour, add a teaspoon of honey, but normally this is unnecessary. Chill before serving.

Caribbean Banana

Something special to do with bananas, especially when the weather is miserable. If you want to be indulgent, you could serve this with cream, but natural yoghurt is healthier.

> 2 bananas
> a sprinkling of raisins
> 1 tsp brown sugar or clear honey
> 1 tsp lemon juice
> dash of orange juice
> dollops of natural yoghurt

Pre-heat the grill. Peel the bananas and slice lengthways. Lay in a heatproof dish. Sprinkle the banana halves with raisins, lemon and orange juice. Finish off with a sprinkling of brown sugar or honey. Cover with foil and grill for 5–10 minutes. At the end, remove the foil for a few minutes. Serve hot with natural yoghurt topping.

Tofu Dessert Whip

Tofu, or soya beancurd, can be used in sweet as well as savoury dishes. Whipped up with fruit it makes a deliciously creamy dessert which is, incidentally, highly nutritious.

> $\frac{1}{2}$ × 285 g/10$\frac{1}{2}$ oz pkt silken tofu
> 1 tsp lemon juice (prevents discolouring)
> 1 tsp vanilla essence
> 1 banana
> 1 tbsp cold water
> 1 lge tsp clear honey

Put all the ingredients together in a blender until smooth. Pour into a serving dish and chill in the fridge.

Dried Fruit Compote

Dried fruits are especially useful in winter and make a delicious fruit salad which is marvellous with yoghurt. Try to buy dried fruits which have not been treated with sulphur dioxide and chemicals to preserve their colour and shelf-life. Many brands of dried fruit are also sprayed with mineral oil, which lessens the body's ability to absorb vitamins. Look for fruits without additives which have been naturally dried. Always rinse fruit before use.

Fruits prepared in this way keep in the fridge for 4 or 5 days; they keep for months if deep frozen.

450 g/1 lb dried fruits – these can be varied, but my combination is as follows:
100 g/4 oz dried figs
150 g/5 oz dried prunes
150 g/5 oz dried apricots
25 g/1 oz raisins
25 g/1 oz sultanas
1 tsp clear honey
1 cinnamon stick
a dash of orange juice
a twist of lemon rind
a pinch ground allspice

Rinse the fruits in cold water. Put them in a bowl, cover with fresh cold water and soak overnight in the fridge. Put the fruit in its soaking water in a saucepan with the honey, cinnamon, allspice and lemon rind. Bring to the boil, reduce the heat and simmer gently for about 10 minutes until the fruits are tender. Take out the cinnamon and lemon rind.

Stir in the orange juice and put the fruit into a serving bowl. Chill in the fridge. If the juice seems too rich, thin down a little with cold water. Serve on its own or topped with natural yoghurt or whipped cream.

Apple and Blackberry Crumble

Apples and blackberries are so delicious together and full of vitamins and minerals. The crumble topping for this recipe can be used on a variety of fruit bases – rhubarb or gooseberries are two alternatives. Since you need to use the oven for this recipe, it serves about 4 portions.

450 g/1 lb cooking apples
100 g/4 oz wholemeal flour
75 g/3 oz unsalted butter or margarine
50 g/2 oz oatflakes
60 g/$2\frac{1}{2}$ oz brown raw cane sugar
1×200 g/7 oz tin blackberries in apple juice
1 tsp allspice

Preheat the oven to GM6/400°F/200°C. Wash, core and thinly slice the apples, leaving the peel on. Put them in a saucepan with the juice from the tin of blackberries, the allspice and $1\frac{1}{2}$ oz sugar. Simmer for about 10 minutes until they are tender but not mushy. Drain off most of the cooking juice, place the apples in an ovenproof dish and mix in the blackberries.

Meanwhile, in a mixing bowl, rub the butter into the flour and oatflakes until you have fine crumbs. Mix in the remaining

1 oz sugar. Put the crumble on top of the apples, pressing down lightly and evenly, then run a fork over surface.

Bake in the oven for about 20–25 minutes and serve hot with cream or yoghurt if desired.

If you use rhubarb, simply trim and cut it into chunks and simmer in a little water over a low heat with sugar for about 5–10 minutes, then top with crumble. With gooseberries, top and tail the berries, and treat as above.

Lhassis and Shakes

As an alternative to a dessert, a thick yoghurt drink or real milk shake can be a delightful change, especially during the warm summer months. Home-made drinks bear little resemblance to the artificial shakes you make up from packets and tins. I simply use fresh seasonal fruits with milk or yoghurt, occasionally adding as a treat a spoonful of good additive-free ice-cream (Loseley ice-creams, though expensive, are certainly worth the money).

Banana Lhassi

The Indians call their yoghurt drinks 'lhassi' and make them both sweet and salty. Made properly, they are wonderfully refreshing in hot weather.

> 1 ripe banana
> 1 small carton of natural yoghurt, beaten
> 1 tsp runny honey
> 2 drops of vanilla essence
> ice cubes

Beat the yoghurt and make it up to $\frac{1}{2}$ pt with cold water. Put this with the other ingredients in a blender. Give it a good whizz and pour into a long glass over some crushed ice cubes.

This basic recipe can be varied by combining milk or yoghurt/ water with different soft fruits. The best are probably pineapple, peaches, strawberries, raspberries and mangoes. Make sure the fruit is really ripe, and you might prefer to strain berries before putting them in the blender to remove the pips. As children get a little older you can experiment with some additional ground nuts as well.

APPENDIX:
ADDITIVES TO
AVOID

The following list includes those additives in food products which are known to have links with intolerant reactions. While it is vital to avoid these ingredients if your child appears hyper-active, has problems with asthma or eczema, or is sensitive to aspirin, I feel that they should if possible be excluded from the diet of all babies and children.

ARTIFICIAL COLOURS

    E102 Tartrazine
    E104 Quinoline Yellow
    E107 Yellow 2G
    E110 Sunset Yellow
    E120 Cochineal
    E122 Carmoisine
    E123 Amaranth
    E124 Ponceau 4R
    E127 Erythrosine
    E128 Red 2G
    E132 Indigo Carmine
    E133 Brilliant Blue
    E150 Caramel
    E151 Black PN
    E154 Brown FK
    E155 Chocolate Brown HT

NATURAL COLOUR

E160b Annatto

PRESERVATIVES

E210—E219 Benzoates
E220—E227 Sulphites
E250 Sodium nitrite
E251 Sodium nitrate

ANTI-OXIDANTS

E310 Propyl gallate
E311 Octyl gallate
E312 Dodecyl gallate
E320 Butylated hydroxyanisole
E321 Butylated hydroxytoluene

FLAVOUR ENHANCERS

621 Sodium hydrogen L-glutamate (Monosodium glutamate; MSG)
622 Potassium hydrogen L-glutamate
623 Calcium dihydrogen di-L-glutamate
627 Guanosine 5'-(disodium phosphate)
631 Ompsome 5'-(disodium phosphate)
635 Sodium 5'-ribonucleotide

SOURCES

Maurice Hanssen, *E for Additives* (1984, Guildford and Kings Lynn, Thorsons), pp. 12—13.
The London Food Commission, *Food Adulteration and How to Beat It* (1988, London, Unwin Paperbacks), p. 52.

INDEX